CHRIST IN YOUR LIFE

Sandy Karstens

WESTBOW
PRESS®
A DIVISION OF THOMAS NELSON
& ZONDERVAN

WestBow Press books may be ordered through booksellers or by contacting:

WestBow Press
A Division of Thomas Nelson & Zondervan
1663 Liberty Drive
Bloomington, IN 47403
www.westbowpress.com
844-714-3454

ISBN: 978-1-6642-2952-5 (sc)
ISBN: 978-1-6642-2953-2 (hc)
ISBN: 978-1-6642-2951-8 (e)

Library of Congress Control Number: 2021906418

Print information available on the last page.

WestBow Press rev. date: 04/23/2021

CONTENTS

DEDICATION

I affectionately dedicate this book to my daughters
Sheila, Paula, Sarah, and Laura.
And to my grandchildren Andrew, Christopher,
Madeline, Alexandra, Taylor and Jaydin.
To Jesus' children who know Him.
And to all His children who will come to know Him.

ACKNOWLEDGMENTS

First and foremost, praises and thank you to my Heavenly Father for His blessings throughout the writing of this book and for successfully bringing it to completion.

Additionally, my special thanks to my daughters and grandchildren. You fill each day with love, laughter and joy. I am praying for you. The Lord has blessed me with dear friends. Thank you for your encouragement, support and assistance in writing this book. And a special thanks to my editor Cindy Jackelen. God placed you in my life with your editing knowledge when I didn't know where to turn. You are a blessing.

INTRODUCTION

You and I are on a journey, a journey through life. I grew up in a Christian home. Growing up in a Christian home meant attending church. My siblings and myself attended Sunday School and Catechism on Wednesday evenings. From my youngest days I knew the name of Jesus. The Bible was in the house but never opened or studied.

Along the way on this journey God called me into a deeper relationship. I chose Christ and wanted to grow as a Christian. I continue to grow in the winter season of life. I have a responsibility to move forward. God calls all of us to take this journey through life. We have a choice. It is our decision to take His road which is narrow or the wide road of this world. Psalm 103:11 declares, "For as high as the heavens are above the earth, so great is his love for those who fear Him." It is easy to have a surface relationship with Him.

My intention for this book is to share my experiences with my children and grandchildren since my life experiences with Christ included them. I share my weaknesses, my sinfulness and my strengths. I am a humble elderly grandmother that has been touched by God. My desire is that the Lord and Holy Spirit will use what I share in your life. My main focus is on His Word, prayer and a walk of faith.

It is my wish you spend time studying the Bible, reading Biblical material and praying. Read not only with your mind but also with your heart. I pray that this book helps you as you travel your journey of faith. You must be open to His presence in everything.

The real lesson is to look within yourself with God's word in hand and prayer.

THE ROAD I AM ON

"For I know the thoughts that I think toward you, saith the LORD, thoughts of peace, and not of evil, to give you an expected end." (Jeremiah 29:11)

1

Now that I am older looking back through my life, it feels as though I have been on one detour after another.

The strongest lesson we can learn from traveling on the roadways of life is it cannot always be straight and smooth. There must be hills, potholes and detours. We have all had the experience of traveling along when suddenly we are confronted with a large sign saying, "Highway Closed. Follow Detour Signs." By following the detour signs, we are brought back to the smooth highway. Life is very much like that.

We can go for months or even years and encounter truly little trouble. Suddenly, we are confronted with a dilemma. It may be one of sorrow, loneliness, illness or grave disappointments. My husband wanted to own a restaurant, so we purchased a local restaurant. My husband closed his insurance agency and I left the realty agency. We both had great anticipation for this new journey. A year and a half into operation of our restaurant, a chain restaurant came into town. Business slowed because everyone wanted to try the new restaurant. Of course, that is to be expected. We were on a shoestring budget. It was difficult to keep the restaurant open until our business returned to normal. We held on as long as we could but decided that we could not keep it open and needed to close the doors. Our home was attached to the business. We walked away with nothing. My mother-in-law opened her home to our four children and us.

We did not anticipate something like this even happening when we purchased the business. The detour appeared without warning. There was no going back. We could grumble about it, be fearful and ashamed. What would people say? That detour was rough, but we pulled it together, accepted it and moved forward. The detour took us through many decisions that were not easy. Some were heartbreaking. We tried to stay calm and peaceful as our world crumbled around us. We prayed and asked God for His guidance and strength. Our faith carried us through, knowing that there must be a purpose for this detour. What attitude would you take towards your detours?

It is easy to feel your path is not taking you to your destination because of all the detours. When God is taking you to your destination, he rarely moves you from where you are to where He wants you to be without taking you on a road trip first. He does not go from A to B to C. He goes from A to Z to T to R to F to D, meandering you through your life.

God took the Israelites on a detour of their own. Exodus.13:17 "When Pharaoh let the people go, God did not lead them on the road through the Philistine country, though that was shorter. For God said, 'If they face war, they might change their minds and return to Egypt.'"

So, God led the people the roundabout way through the wilderness toward the Red Sea. It may not make sense to us, but God has a reason for our detours. God wants us to come closer to Him. While feeling worried, fearful or threatened, we can trust that God is right there with us. Through these detours, we should glorify God with our witnessing. It strengthens our faith.

God uses detours to build our hope and trust in God and secure our heavenly home. As believers, we will be with Christ in eternity; we will realize that life on earth was one big detour!

NARROW PATH OR THE WIDE PATH TO THE GATE OF HEAVEN

"Enter through the narrow gate. For wide is the gate and broad is the road that leads to destruction, and many enter through it. But small is the gate and narrow the road that leads to life, and only a few find it" (Matthew 7:13-14).

T hroughout the Bible, God makes it known that the house of
God continues to be the gate of Heaven. In my life, I ask myself
many times, "Will I go to Heaven? The question "Where will I
go when I die?" It is important to me and to many others. "Jesus
answered, "I am the way and the truth and the life. No one comes to
the Father except through me." (John 14:6) It was Elijah, the great
prophet, who called for a decision. "Elijah went before the people and
said, "How long will you waver between two opinions? If the Lord is
God follow Him, but if Baal is God, follow him." (1 Kings 18:21)

Picture this. You are walking along on a road with others and the
road comes to a division. Let us say one road goes left and is narrow
and the other goes right and is broad. They both have gates. You notice
the broad road is well worn. The majority of people before you go
through the wide gate. It looks inviting and pleasant. It is tempting to
join the others. You think, "These people must know that this is the
right way to go."

The narrow road has ruts, boulders and drop-offs on both sides.
You stand there and look at both gates with their paths. You need to
choose. As you look through the broad gate, the path would certainly
make you feel good. We like what makes us feel good. We do not like
anything that is difficult in our lives. As you look at the narrow gate
and its difficult road, you wonder why you should choose this narrow
path to travel with all its challenges.

God warns us about this broad road. Why should this be of
concern to us? It is in Genesis Chapter 3 that Adam relinquished his
authority of the earth to Satan. Satan assumed dominion over the
earth. "Therefore, just as sin entered the world through one man, and
death through sin, and in this way death came to all people, because
all sinned—." (Romans 5:12) Thankfully, one day God will remove
Satan from the earth. The Bible says when Jesus Christ returns at His
Second Coming, He will bind all evil spirits. God has given us free
will whereby we can choose to follow the world and its ways or follow
Jesus Christ. "On that day a fountain will be opened to the house of
David and the inhabitants of Jerusalem, to cleanse them from sin

and impurity. "On that day, I will banish the names of the idols from the land, and they will be remembered no more," declares the LORD Almighty. "I will remove both the prophets and the spirit of impurity from the land." (Zachariah 13:1,2)

The second part of the scripture. "But small is the gate and narrow the road that leads to life, and only a few find it." The narrow path is the road of a Christian life. It is difficult but it leads to life. It is the beginning not the end. Even though we have challenges in our lives, we must choose to follow Jesus. We must avoid the wide gate and the wide path. They lead to our destruction. You cannot get to Heaven by being good. Take up your cross, love God with all your heart and bear rejection courageously. Be among the few who find life. "Anyone who loves their father or mother more than me is not worthy of me; anyone who loves their son or daughter more than me is not worthy of me. Whoever does not take up their cross and follow me is not worthy of me. Whoever finds their life will lose it, and whoever loses their life for my sake will find it." (Matthew 10:37-39) "Give careful thought to the paths for your feet and be steadfast in all your ways." (Proverbs 4:26)

A man died and went to heaven. As he stood in front of the gate to Heaven, he was told, "The gate is closed." "Therefore, Jesus said again, 'Very truly I tell you, I am the gate for the sheep. All who have come before Me are thieves and robbers, but the sheep have not listened to them. I am the gate; whoever enters through Me will be saved. They will come in and go out and find pasture. The thief comes only to steal and kill and destroy; I have come that they may have life and have it to the full." (John 10:7-10)

On one of my trips, I did not make my connecting flight in Charlotte, NC. My flight out of Minneapolis was delayed 40 minutes and I only had a short layover in Charlotte. When I arrived in Charlotte, I was told the concourse for my next flight was on the other side of the terminal. I secured a motorized cart and told the driver my flight information and we needed to hurry. The young man called the gate and told them we were on our way. They told him that they had closed the gate. I would need to secure a different flight.

Do you want to be at the gate of Heaven and told, "The gate is closed?" When I did get my new boarding pass and waited to load the next flight, I thought about how I felt being just minutes from the gate and told the gate would not be opening for me to board. The gate was closed. What a sinking feeling I had. I could do nothing to open the gate. I do not want to be at the gate of Heaven and be told, *"THE GATE IS CLOSED."*

So, will it be the Broad or the Narrow...What Path Will You Choose?
For your life depends on it.

TOMORROW IS GOD'S SECRET, BUT TODAY IS YOURS TO LIVE

"Why, you do not even know what will happen tomorrow. What is your life? You are a mist that appears for a little while and then vanishes." (James 4:14)

God presents each new day for us to use as we may. As we begin each day, we accept that yesterday is gone. Paul wrote in Philippians 3:13, "Brothers and sisters, I do not consider myself yet to have taken hold of it. But one thing I do: Forgetting what is behind and straining toward what is ahead..."

There is the reality of our present moment, our today. How will we use it? We can spend it on ourselves, on some cherished plan or desire of our own. Or we can ask our heavenly Father to use us for His will. Today is a privilege for us and a special gift from God. Why waste time brooding or longing over the past? It is gone. And why be fearful of tomorrow? It may never come.

I am not exempt from worrying about the past or worrying about the future. It seems that my thoughts go to worrying more often than I want them to. It seems to take a trial in life for us to stop and think about what is important. I have four daughters. My third eldest had four cardiac arrests and a stroke when she was in her early forties. The doctors stated they would do what they could, but it might quickly go the other way. I said, "The other way!". We prayed and reached out to our families, friends, church families, prayer groups and many others.

Each day we received positive words from the doctors. We saw God's power in her weak body. In prayer this scripture came to mind. He said to me, "My grace is sufficient for you, for my power is made perfect in weakness. Therefore, I will boast all the more gladly about my weaknesses, so that Christ's power may rest on me." (2 Corinthians 12: 9) There is no doubt in my mind that her recovery is a miracle.

We talked about how one day she was fine, and the next she was fighting for her life. We were scared we would not have a tomorrow with her. We soon realized that our need was to face each day, not what was yesterday, nor what will be tomorrow. What was God going to do today? How can we praise our God today? How can we tell others about what God is doing here today?

This present moment is a special gift from God. We are to be still and listen to His voice. He will reveal how we are to spend each day.

When life is going well for us, it is easy to feel hopeful for our tomorrows. But when our world falls apart, we lose hope. These moments are a special gift from God. Thankfully, the hope that God offers is much more than a feeling. It is the reality of His presence.

David wrote, "Show me, Lord, my life's end and the number of my days let me know how fleeting my life is. You have made my days a mere handbreadth; the span of my years is as nothing before you. Everyone is but a breath, even those who seem secure. Surely everyone goes around like a mere phantom; in vain they rush about, heaping up wealth without knowing whose it will finally be. But now, Lord, what do I look for." (Psalm 39:4-7)

Unexpected Journey Leads Us to God's Hope.

SIMPLIFY... FOR JESUS' SAKE

"But godliness with contentment is great gain. For we brought nothing into the world, and we can take nothing out of it. But if we have food and clothing, we will be content with that." (1 Timothy 6:6-8)

What is an important antidote to the "too much stuff" of our culture and the price our precious children are paying for this accumulation of stuff? We have distorted Jesus' declaration, "The thief comes only to steal and kill and destroy; I have come that they may have life and have it to the full." (John 10:10) We have replaced the abundance and the fullness of life, now and forever, --that Jesus promised --with too many things, too many choices and a life that moves too fast. It is a world of physical and mental clutter. We have muffled our ears so we do not hear Jesus declare, "For where your treasure is, there will your heart be also." (Matthew 6:21)

What is the "treasure" you want for your child? Childhood is a season of grace, filled with imagination, exploration, delight and adventure. We have lost the natural rhythm of the gentle unfolding of childhood in our headlong rush to fill up our children's schedules, build their college resumes and make sure they experience everything. Our children are like flowers. As the flower grows, so do our children. To keep the flower prospering, we need to plant it in good soil, fertilize it, water it and be sure it gets the required sunlight. Nourish your children with praise, compliment them each day and water them with love. Be their sun. Protect them from storms. *We must take care of our children.* Think about the natural rhythm unfolding their childhood.

Kim John Payne is an Australian who for twenty-four years worked as a counselor, consultant and educator of both children and adults. In his book, *Power of Less to Raise Calmer, Happier, and More Secure Kids,* he writes about today's busier, faster society and how it is waging an undeclared war on childhood. With too much stuff, too many choices and too little time, our children can become anxious. They may have trouble with friends and school. They may even be diagnosed with behavioral problems, physical and mental health issues, paying a price none of us ever intended.

Payne suggests some wonderful ways of simplifying life for our children, to recapture the gifts of childhood. How much time is there for children to use their imagination, and play with other children without jerseys, coaches and referees? How much time may they daydream, pretend or explore nature? Let us protect blocks of time on the calendar for those vitally important parts of childhood. Allow our children to get lost in their thoughts. Allow them to hang out with their families. Be aware of the commitments our children are involved in. Fewer endeavors result in deeper engagement, better focus and sustained involvement. Children are more peaceful, centered and attentive. They are happier.

I grew up on a farm and worked in the field with my dad. My sister helped our mother in the house and the tending of the animals. But I remember one important activity my sister and I did when we were not busy working. We laid on the grass and gazed at the sky. As clouds came across the sky, we would tell each other what image we saw in them. We want our children to find peaceful activities that they will treasure.

And how about the "stuff" that is the earmark of an American childhood? Where did it all come from? Why do we hold onto it? Where do we store it? In many households, children's technology, toys and electronic devices have taken on a life of their own. The overabundant supply of possessions gets in the way of a child's ability to see what is there to play with. It distracts and overwhelms our children. We must make sure we select the things of value, *lest our possessions own us.*

It is in being still, in quieting the roar of cultural demands and desires when we experience the living God and cherish one another.

"Be still and know that I am God." (Psalm 46:10)

NO GRIEF OVER OLD MISTAKES

"The Lord is not slow in keeping His promise, as some understand slowness. Instead He is patient with you, not wanting anyone to perish, but everyone to come to repentance." (2 Peter 3:9)

n a short meditation, I read, "I am a work in progress. Sorry for any inconvenience caused." There is no one living who, at the beginning of a new year cannot recall mistakes made during the old year. We may deeply regret some of them.

What shall we do with these past mistakes? Shall we continue to worry about them throughout the year that the Lord has given us? Or shall we forget them and pretend they never happened? Or shall we learn all we can from them and face the year joyously, in the full confidence of God's forgiveness?

I doubt that our heavenly Father wants us to grieve too long over old mistakes. He wants us to learn from them and try to avoid them in the future.

Herbie Hancock, born April 12, 1940, is an American pianist, keyboardist, bandleader and composer. Early in his career, Miles Davis invited Herbie to play in his quintet. Miles was already a musical legend. During one performance, when Davis was near the high point of his solo, Herbie played the wrong chord. Herbie was mortified, but Davis continued as if nothing had happened. "He played some notes that made my chord right," Herbie said.

Taken from Our Daily Bread®, Copyright©, 2015
by Our Daily Bread Ministries, Grand Rapids, MI
Reprinted by permission. All rights reserved.

What an example of loving leadership! Davis did not scold Herbie or make him look foolish. He did not blame him for ruining the performance. He simply adjusted his plan and turned a potentially disastrous mistake into something beautiful. It took Herbie years to realize Miles did not judge the chord, Herbie did.

What Davis did for Herbie, Jesus did for Peter. When Peter cut off the ear of one of the individuals in the crowd who had come to arrest Jesus, Jesus reattached the ear (Luke 22:51). By healing the ear, Jesus indicated His kingdom was about healing, not hurting. Time after time, Jesus used the disciples' mistakes to show a better way.

What Jesus did for His disciples, He also does for us. God works through our mistakes. God does not waste these experiences because He will turn them into something good. God directs us through our mistakes. Some of my biggest mistakes taught me powerful lessons and revealed to me a new direction and or a change. People are like teabags. If you want to know what is really inside a person, drop them into hot water. How we respond to mistakes, problems and sin tests the strength of our faith. "Consider it pure joy, my brothers and sisters, whenever you face trials of many kinds, because you know that the testing of your faith produces perseverance." (James 1:2-3)

Lessons are not learned in the light. It is in the darkness that God corrects us. I have found God in this darkness of pain and defeat. Have you found Him? God draws us closer to Him in our pain. Have you ever made a mistake that turned out to be a blessing in disguise? God protects us through these mistakes. When we respond correctly to the mistakes, they build our character. He has perfected us.

And what He does for us, we can do for others. Instead of magnifying every mistake, we can turn them into beautiful acts of forgiveness, healing and redemption.

Do not be afraid to make mistakes.
Be afraid of not learning from them.

THE GIFT OF LOVE...FAMILY

"And now these three remain: faith, hope and love. But the greatest of these is love." (1 Corinthians 13:13)

The ultimate love story is the love our God has for us when sending Jesus into the world. Love is our greatest need as humans. With God's love in our hearts, we are prompted and enabled to love others. We have our own "love stories." Our love stories are the most significant part of our lives.

We all come from families. The first question to ask is, who is my family? God instituted family. "The LORD God said, "It is not good for the man to be alone. I will make a helper suitable for him." (Genesis 2:18) You are brought into a family by birth. We are also brought into His Christian family. "See what great love the Father has lavished on us, that we should be called children of God! And that is what we are! The reason the world does not know us is that it did not know Him." (1 John 3:1)

In families, we learn caring, serving and customs. Family teaches us about love. Sometimes the world beats us up, but it is in the family we find and learn love and acceptance. "Accept one another, then, just as Christ accepted you, in order to bring praise to God." (Romans 15:7)

How did Christ accept us? Love. He asks for love and He gives love. We need families where we can heal from the trials of the world. "Therefore, confess your sins to one another, and pray for one another so that you may be healed. The prayer of a righteous person is powerful and effective." (James 5:16) Sometimes pride gets in the way of asking family for help. As death comes to a family, we grieve with each other, and we wait for each other when moving through grief. As a family, we support each other through trials.

No family is perfect and family relationships can shatter. God understands this. What God wants us to do is to repent and forgive, keep loving your family and trust God to be God. We cannot fix things. God must fix things.

The Bible covers two types of love, agape and phileo. Agape love is represented by God's love and commitment to us. A true illustration of this requires a relationship with Christ. For without Him, agape love is not in its truest form. We, as humans, cannot reach this level alone. We need the Holy Spirit in us, working through us.

The other kind of love is phileo. Phileo is considered "brotherly love" friendship. It is usually based on how others treat us and our feelings in any given situation. It involves direct interaction. Sometimes it can come with a price tag of expectation, wanting something back in return. It is also a command from God. "Dear friends, let us love one another, for love comes from God. Everyone who loves has been born of God and knows God." (1 John 4:7)

The relationships in our lives will either be agape or phileo love. When thinking in terms of romance, we allow the manifestation of the agape love to pour out from our hearts. We are eager to do everything we can to please the other person and make that person happy. "That is why a man leaves his father and mother and is united to his wife, and they become one flesh." (Genesis 2:24) The best book in the Bible on romantic and agape type of love is the Song of Solomon. Every passage attests to the deep and abiding love between the lover and beloved.

With what kind of love does God love us? So often, I think about how much God loves me. I ask myself, "How can God love me?" It is hard to comprehend this kind of love. His love is all-encompassing. He not only loves the nicest or popular people, but those individuals who society leaves behind. God's love is sacrificial. God gave His Son to die on the cross. God's love is steadfast, non-moveable. God's love is personal. We have a personal relationship with God.

"For God so loved the world that He gave His one
and only Son, that whoever believes in Him shall not
perish but have eternal life." (John 3:16)

THE GIFT OF LOVE…FRIENDS

"And now these three remain: faith, hope, and love. But the greatest of these is love." (1 Corinthians 13:13)

When we turn our focus to God, we can offer great encouragement and hope to those in need. When we are willing to enter into the pain of a suffering friend, we follow the example of Jesus. "Rejoice with those who rejoice and mourn with those who mourn." (Romans 12:15) Jesus came to bear our pain and suffer in our place. Our help to those in need is ultimately a way we serve Christ. "The King will reply, 'Truly I tell you, whatever you did for one of the least of these brothers and sisters of mine, you did for me.'" (Matthew 25:40)

Friendships are important to God. Through friendships we counsel, support and share our lives. Friendships influence our lives. It is important to follow God's guidance in establishing friendships. "Above all, love each other deeply, because love covers over a multitude of sins." (1 Peter 4:8)

You can look at friendship as four levels: 1) acquaintance, 2) casual friendship, 3) close friendship and 4) intimate friendship. Acquaintance is a relationship that is occasional. Casual friendships can develop quickly as you discover common interests, activities and concerns. It involves a oneness of soul (the mind, will, and emotions). A close friendship reflects oneness of spirit. It requires that both persons share the same life goals. The deepest level of friendship is intimate friendship. This is when you invest in each other's lives and help each other. Honesty, humility and discretion are requirements of an intimate friendship. Comfort one another through trials and sorrows and pray diligently for one another.

One of the famous friendships in the Bible is Jonathan, King Saul's son, and David. They were not Facebook friends or schoolmates. They were not men who interacted now and then. David and Jonathan had a deep, meaningful relationship; they loved each other. Jonathan's deep relationship with David grew even if David was to become King because Saul favored him.

David and Jonathan sacrificed for one another. 1 Samuel 18:4, "Jonathan took off the robe he was wearing and gave it to David, along with his tunic, and even his sword, his bow, and his belt." The significance of this gift was that Jonathan recognized that David would one day be king of Israel. Rather than being envious or jealous, Jonathan submitted to God's will and sacrificed his own right to the throne. When King Saul wanted to kill David, Jonathan put his own life in danger. Sometimes being a true Christian friend means we need to make sacrifices for our friends. Are we willing to share things that are important to us? Are we willing to sacrifice time, money, our life for our friends? Jesus made the ultimate sacrifice by laying down His life for us.

Jonathan was willing to be in the shadows. During the years that David was in hiding from Saul, Jonathan always found a way to see David. On one of his visits, Jonathan said to David, "Don't be afraid," he said. "My father Saul will not lay a hand on you. You will be king over Israel, and I will be second to you. Even my father Saul knows this." (1 Samuel 23:17) Jonathan was willing to live in the shadow so that David could reign. How good are we at stepping into the shadows?

We should stand up for our friends. Jonathan defended David before his father, Saul. "Jonathan spoke well of David to Saul his father and said to him, "Let not the king do wrong to his servant David; he has not wronged you, and what he has done has benefited you greatly. He took his life in his hands when he killed the Philistine. The LORD won a great victory for all Israel, and you saw it and were glad. Why then would you do wrong to an innocent man like David by killing him for no reason." (1 Samuel 19:4-5)

We need the freedom to be ourselves. Jonathan went to David after knowing that Saul asked someone to bring David back. David was to be killed. "After the boy had gone, David got up from the south side of the stone and bowed down before Jonathan three times, with his face to the ground. Then they kissed each other and wept together—but David wept the most." (1 Samuel 20:41) Can you openly share your sorrows with a friend? Be yourself without judgment?

A sweet friendship refreshes our soul. Job's three friends were Eliphaz, Bildad and Zophar. Job's three friends agree on some points in Job's situation, but there are differences among them.

Job 2:11-13, "When Job's three friends, Eliphaz the Temanite, Bildad the Shuhite and Zophar the Naamathite, heard about all the troubles that had come upon him, they set out from their homes and met together by agreement to go and sympathize with him and comfort him. When they saw him from a distance, they could hardly recognize him; they began to weep aloud, and they tore their robes and sprinkled dust on their heads. Then they sat on the ground with him for seven days and seven nights. No one said a word to him because they saw how great his suffering was."

Job's friends did at least three things right. First, they came to him when he was suffering. Second, they empathized with him. "They began to weep aloud, and they tore their robes and sprinkled dust on their heads." (verse 12) Third, they spent time with him. Verse 13 states they were with him for seven days before they offered their advice. They expressed the sympathy with their friend Job.

But their silence did not last forever and these three men gave a series of speeches to Job. (Job:4-25) The speeches of Job's three friends include many inaccuracies, primarily involving why God allows people to suffer. Their belief was that Job was suffering because he had done something wrong. As a result, they repeatedly encourage Job to admit his wrong and repent so that God would bless him again.

God clearly condemned their advice. "After the LORD had said these things to Job, he said to Eliphaz the Temanite, "I am angry with you and your two friends, because you have not spoken the truth about me, as my servant Job has." (Job 42:7) Though, in the end, Job was mistaken in overstating his righteousness. He had done nothing to deserve his suffering. The trials Job endured were not related to his behavior. Instead, God used the sufferings as a test and as part of His sovereign plan in Job's life. Following Job's time of suffering, God blessed Job with twice as much as he had before.

Much can be learned from the example of Job and his friends. When we are aware of a friend who is hurting, we can follow the positive example of these men by going to the person, mourning with him and spending time together. Our physical presence with a hurting

31

friend can be a great comfort in and of itself, even if we have no words to say.

In addition, we can gain wisdom from what Job's friends did wrong. We should not assume that troubles are the sure sign of God's judgment. "As he went along, he saw a man blind from birth. His disciples asked Him, "Rabbi, who sinned, this man or his parents, that he was born blind?" "Neither this man nor his parents sinned," said Jesus, "but this happened so that the works of God might be displayed in Him." (John 9:1-3)

Instead of telling a hurting person to admit his wrong and repent when we do not know the reason for the suffering, we can join together and encourage a friend to endure faithfully. We know God sees our pain and has a purpose for it.

"Two are better than one, they have a good return for their labor: If either of them falls down, one can help the other up. But pity anyone who falls and has no one to help them up. Also, if two lie down together, they will keep warm. But how can one keep warm alone? Though one may be overpowered, two can defend themselves." (Ecclesiastes 4:9-12) We need friendship.

My story of friendship includes six ladies and me. We worked for the same company. The company's transportation department had a fleet of commuter vans. I drove one of those vans and picked up and dropped off these friends for years. And through those years, we supported each other during difficult times and celebrated the joys in each of our lives. We lost one friend to cancer and one friend moved to California after her daughter died from cancer. When I say a friend is someone who comes in when others left, this is so true. Others would drift away, but we stood by each other. We continue being committed to each other. These friends are God's blessed gift to me. I cherish their friendship forevermore.

As a quiet, shy and reserved individual it has not always been easy for me to find valued friendships. How should we seek friends? God desires us to have friends. We should pray for valued friendships. Be that love-filled friend and commit yourself to your friendships. Be God's gift to someone and be the friend first.

Do not walk in front of me; I may not follow.
Do not walk behind me; I may not lead.
Just walk beside me and be my friend. – Albert Camus.

WHO IS YOUR NEIGHBOR?
(PARABLE OF THE GOOD SAMARITAN)

"But he wanted to justify himself, so he asked Jesus,
'And who is my neighbor?'" (Luke 10:29)

We commonly think of neighbors as the people who live near us, but Jesus meant it to include all humanity. Jesus told His famous parable of the Good Samaritan to make it clear that "love your neighbor" means to love all persons, everywhere, not just our family, friends, neighbors and community in which we live.

In the parable, Jesus does something different. Right at the end, He does not ask who was the Samaritan's neighbor? Rather He asks who acted like a neighbor? The answer, of course, is obvious to the lawyer and us. It is the Samaritan, the one who went out of his way to help another. But do you notice how this changes things? Suddenly the neighbor is not simply the one in need, but rather the one who provides for our need, the one who takes care of us.

This parable is all about love. So, along with the lawyer, we try to figure out who we are supposed to love. While reading this parable, my focus went to the man at the side of the road who needed help; he was the neighbor. Jesus turned this around in the parable. Who acted in mercy? Think about it. As John Piper, author, speaker and chancellor of Bethlehem College & Seminary in Minneapolis, MN explains, "When we are done trying to establish, 'Is this my neighbor?' — the decisive issue of love remains. "What kind of person am I?"

God expects us to care for our neighbor and to see anyone in need as our neighbor. Are we a loving neighbor? Who are you? — that is the question. The Samaritan in Jesus' story did not just do something; he felt something. "But a Samaritan, as he traveled came to where the man was; and when he saw him, he took pity on him." (Luke 10:33) If you read earlier in the passage, you see that this whole story was told to illustrate the fact that the greatest command for anyone who wants to follow Jesus is about love.

The priest and the Levite did not see the man in the ditch as their neighbor but as a burden. Are we going to be like the Samaritan who gives help when help is needed? Or are we going to be caught up in questions about who we are supposed to help? You may ask yourself, "What if it will make me late for church." The parable is also about excuses, self-justification and about letting oneself off the hook. The

Good Samaritan did not give his spare change to fill an empty whiskey bottle. When I have helped a needy person, I have been asked, "How do you know they are not using it to buy alcohol or drugs?" Are there qualifiers that should be our guide in helping individuals? Maybe? We get caught up in who is poor and when help can hurt. These are important questions. We should think about them. But while we think, may we never lose sight that the central issue has to do with LOVE.

The issue here is love and compassion. We can make ourselves help the man in the ditch, but can we make ourselves love him? We do not manufacture love. Knowing the right thing to do, we then do something, but we cannot force ourselves to love those in need. If we want to go and do likewise truly, we cannot just help. We also must feel.

We all have neighbors, but it is important to remember that we are neighbors also. Sometimes we may be the one in need of care. We should be open to it as much as we hope our neighbors are open to our care. It is a mutual blessing.

What determines the way we think about neighbors is who we are, not who are we. What matters first is who we are. Whatever the lawyer had in mind for the answer, it was not the story that Jesus told. "The King will reply, 'Truly I tell you, whatever you did for one of the least of these brothers and sisters of mine, you did for me.'" (Matthew 25:40)

It is so much harder when love has to put shoes on — when we have to walk in those words. Who needs your love today?

THE GIFT OF PEACE

"Peace I leave with you; my peace I give you. I do not give to you as the world gives. Do not let your hearts be troubled and do not be afraid." (John 14:27)

The New Testament speaks of two kinds of peace—the peace that has to do with our relationship to God and the peace that has to do with our experience in life.

When we are born, we lack peace with God. We all come into the world fighting against God because we are a part of the rebellion that started with Adam and Eve. Romans 5:10 says we were enemies of God. We can receive the Son, Jesus Christ, as our Savior by personal faith. "But to all who have received him--those who believe in his name--he has given the right to become God's children." (John 1:12)

When we receive Jesus Christ, we cease being enemies of God. Jesus gave us this peace with His blood on the cross. Jesus said, "Peace I leave with you; my peace I give you. I do not give to you as the world gives. Do not let your hearts be troubled and do not be afraid." (John 14:27) He had also told His followers, "I have told you these things, so that in me you may have peace. In this world you will have trouble. But take heart! I have overcome the world." (John 16:33)

Romans 5:1 says, "Therefore, since we have been justified through faith, we have peace with God through our Lord Jesus Christ." We who trust Christ are redeemed and declared righteous by faith. Our sins are forgiven, rebellion ceases, the war is over and we have peace with God. That was God's wonderful purpose in salvation.

After Adam and Eve did not follow God's command, God was on one side and we were on the other. God sent His Son, Jesus Christ, to bring us to Him so that by repenting and asking for forgiveness, we can walk with God eternally. Christ filled the gap between man and God.

The Holy Spirit is the Giver of this peace. He dispenses it as a gift. Galatians 5:22 says one aspect of the fruit of the Spirit is peace. You might ask if it was Christ's peace, why is the Holy Spirit giving it? The answer is in John 16:14, which says, "He will glorify me because it is from me that he will receive what he will make known to you." When Jesus left, He said He would leave a Helper. The helper was the Holy Spirit. So, all that is Christ will be given to us by the Holy Spirit.

The only peace this world can know is empty and it changes with circumstances. Most people's pursuit of peace is only an attempt to get away from problems. That is why people seek peace through material possessions, alcohol or other forms of escape. The fact is, apart from God, there is no real peace in this world. The peace of putting your blinders on, of going to bed and forgetting it, is worthless. And yet people try desperately to hold on to this kind of mock peace.

Jesus shows us the proper response to His promise of peace. "Do not let your heart be troubled, nor let it be fearful." (John 14:27) We should be able to take hold of this peace. It is there, it is ours but we must take hold of it. Interestingly, He says, "I give you peace," then He says, "Do not let your heart be troubled." We must take this peace that He gives us, and we must apply it in our lives. When we do, we have the promise of His peace. We will have calm in any storm or circumstance that comes our way.

The peace of Christ is a great resource in helping us to know the will of God. Do you have a problem or a decision to make? Let the peace of Christ make that decision for you. Prepare your action or decision by meditating on God's word. If you find yourself retaining His peace in your heart, do it with the confidence it is God's will. But if you find you do not have a sense of peace and God's blessing about it, do not do it.

Sin destroys your sense of peace. It breaks our communion with God. Sin is offensive to God. Perfect peace comes when our focus is off the problem, off the trouble and constantly on Christ. Isaiah 26:3 says, "You will keep in perfect peace those whose minds are steadfast because they trust in you."

The world today is continuously a society in which we are bombarded with advertising and other worldly pressures designed to get us to focus on our needs and problems. How can we keep our minds focused on Christ? By studying the Word of God and asking the Holy Spirit to help us fix our hearts on Jesus Christ.

One winter a friend and I drove to Florida. On our way we also stopped to visit Barb, my sister-in-law in North Carolina. My friend flew home after a week. I spent a month with Barb. Then I drove to

Florida alone. The trip went well and I arrived safely at my friend's home in Florida. I was there for a month. The time came when I needed to think about getting back home. My new townhome was available for me to move into. I was okay with the nine-hour drive from North Carolina to Florida, but this trip would take twenty-two plus hours on the road, alone.

I was feeling anxious about this trip. Never have I driven so far alone, much less across the country. I prayed and asked God for guidance and His will for me. There were thoughts of being tired, driving through busy cities and the most fear was the unknown. Would I be safe? In the days ahead of leaving I continued in prayer, faith and trusting my God. I had only God to rely on to help me drive home. "In their hearts humans plan their course, but the LORD establishes their steps." (Proverbs 16:9)

In the days just before leaving a peace came upon me. I felt this peace and felt comfortable heading out alone. *My faith was in my Lord.* The trip was a success and I made it home with the help of God.

The source of true peace, Jesus Christ.

DO YOU LOVE ME?

"Love is patient, love is kind. It does not envy, it does not boast, it is not proud. It does not dishonor others, it is not self-seeking, it is not easily angered, it keeps no record of wrongs. Love does not delight in evil but rejoices with the truth. It always protects, always trusts, always hopes, always perseveres." (1 Corinthians 13:4-7)

n the musical 'Fiddler on the Roof,' Golde and Tevye were married; however, they did not know each other until their wedding day. After 25 years, Tevye asks Goldie, "Do you love me?" Tevye asks this again and again. Goldie names all the things she has done for him the last 25 years, and Goldie says, "If that's not loving you, what is?" They agree they love each other and "It's nice to know." Jesus is asking more from us.

How do we answer when God asks, "Do you love me?" "Love the Lord your God with all your heart and with all your soul and with all your strength and with all your mind and, 'Love your neighbor as yourself.'" (Luke 10:27)

The Bible teaches us this in 1 John 4:9-10: "This is how God showed his love among us: He sent his one and only Son into the world that we might live through Him. This is love: not that we loved God, but that He loved us and sent His Son as an atoning sacrifice for our sins." Does God love me? I must confess I sometimes struggle to understand God's love for me. I tell myself I know He loves me. He does, for in the scripture it teaches us that He does. It is one thing to know in our minds and it is another thing to believe it in our hearts.

I have done bad things in my life. I have been disrespectful and other things I am not proud of. I ask myself, "How can God love me? I am a sinner." In the Gospel of John, the barrier for Thomas was his doubt and refusal to believe. He had not been with the disciples the first time Jesus had appeared to them. All Thomas had was their word that Jesus had risen from the dead, but that was not enough for him. He wanted to see Jesus for himself and to touch his wounds. Jesus knows how much we love Him, even in our questions and doubts. All He asks is that we try to fix our hearts on Him, and then that love will well up within us. His love is strong enough to restore you, sustain you and move you into the world as His ambassador.

Jesus drew the same kind of love out of Peter when He talked with him on the shore. (John 21:15-19) Three times, He asked Peter, "Do you love me?" Once for each time that Peter had denied Him. And each time, Peter answered, "Yes."

Jesus did not ask why Peter had abandoned Him. He did not rebuke Peter for his weak faith. He just told him to get back to work and all was forgiven. It was as if it had never happened. This is the kind of love that Jesus wants us to experience as well, especially when we feel as if we have failed Him. He never condemns us for our past faults. Instead, He takes the time to address our needs, our fears, our doubts and our moments of weakness. Then simply and gently, he wipes it all away.

Love is the last word. As much as Jesus' love for those two disciples helped draw them to deeper faith, something else happened as well. Jesus drew love out of them. In those tender encounters, Jesus showed both Thomas and Peter that love is greater than sin. Both those apostles learned that sin is never the last word. Love is always the last word!

Love raises our sights. Jesus sought out Peter and reaffirmed his calling to be a shepherd of the flock. Jesus had enough confidence in Peter to entrust him with the role of feeding his sheep. In his guilt and shame over having denied the Lord, Peter may have retreated to the margins, but Jesus did not let him stay there. Likewise, with Thomas, Jesus welcomed him back with open arms. It is amazing how doubt and guilt can cause us to lower our expectations and turn our focus inward. Do not let your shortcomings keep you from serving your family, your church and the needy.

If we want to love like Jesus, we need to step away from ourselves and see others and their needs. We need to open our hearts and our minds. This opens us up to vulnerability. It is a misconception that when you love with your heart like Jesus, you become a doormat, a wimp. We are no one's doormat. We are sons and daughters of the *Most High God*. "See what great love the Father has lavished on us, that we should be called children of God! And that is what we are! The reason the world does not know us is that it did not know him." (John 3:1)

Observe how Christ loved us and love like that.

THERE'S NO GETTING OVER ME

"For the Son of Man came to seek out and to save the lost." (Luke 19:10)

"No Getting Over Me" by Ronnie Milsap
I'll be the bill you forgot to pay,
I'll be the dream that keeps you awake
I'll be the face that you see in the crowd,
I'll be the times that you cry out loud,
be the smile when there's no one around,
I'll be the book that you just can't put down,
There ain't no getting over me.

When I listen to songs, I sometimes place God in the song. Of course, there certainly are songs with which you cannot do this, but you would be surprised how many you can. One of those songs is the song above.

When God created us, He gave us free will so that we could make our own choices. God is always with us whether we choose Him or not. Sometimes we choose to walk a different path. There is no getting over Him because God is always reaching out to us.

We want to be free to come and go as we please, do as we want. When thinking about following God, our thoughts lead us to feel that we are not free to do as we want. God has given us choices. The choice is ours. We can choose to follow Him or not.

Jesus teaches us His freedom and His joy. In John 10:10 it says we will have joy abundantly.

I will be the bill you forgot to pay; I will be the dream that keeps you awake; I will be the song on the radio; I will be the reason that you tell the boys no. Notice your feelings and desires that you experience at various times, be they worry over your financial situation or you wake up with thoughts of desperation. Instead of worrying or running from those feelings, let them motivate you to pursue time with God because He is there in those circumstances. "Do not be anxious about anything, but in every situation, by prayer and petition, with thanksgiving, present your requests to God. And the peace of God, which transcends all understanding, will guard your hearts and your minds in Christ Jesus." (Philippians 4:6-7)

I will be the face that you see in the crowd. I will be the times that you cry out loud. I will be the smile when there is no one around. I will be the book that you just can't put down. God is all we need for any challenge that may come our way. No person or circumstance can ever remove us from the presence of our loving God. He is always with us, hearing our cries for help, protecting us from danger and watching what we do. He is our ever-present God, Savior, Lord and Master, our dearest friend. "...and teaching them to obey everything I have commanded

you. And surely I am with you always, to the very end of the age."
(Matthew 28:20)

*"The Lord your God is with you, a Mighty Warrior who saves, He
will take great delight in you, and His love He will no longer rebuke
you, but will rejoice over you with singing." (Zephaniah 3:17)*

YOU MEAN YOU WANT ME!

"Once again Jesus went out beside the lake. A large crowd came to Him, and He began to teach them. As He walked along, he saw Levi son of Alphaeus sitting at the tax collector's booth. "Follow me," Jesus told him, and Levi got up and followed Him." (Mark 2:13-14)

While Jesus was having dinner at Levi's house, many tax collectors and sinners were eating with Him and His disciples, for there were many who followed Him. When the Pharisees, teachers of the law, saw Him eating with the sinners and tax collectors, they asked His disciples, "Why does He eat with tax collectors and sinners?" "On hearing this, Jesus said to them, "It is not the healthy who need a doctor, but the sick. I have not come to call the righteous, but sinners." (Mark 2:15-17)

There are times I feel so inadequate because of the sinner I am. I ask myself, "How can God love me? How can God pardon me, a sinner?" I do not deserve His love, His mercy or His grace. It often brings me to tears. How can someone love me so much?

When Jesus saw Matthew, Jesus must have seen how the people despised this tax collector. Jesus felt compassion for Matthew right away. Matthew probably noticed how Jesus was looking at him in a way no one had ever looked at him before. Jesus did not look at him with hate and contempt. Jesus simply looked at him with care.

Matthew was a dishonest tax collector. Most tax collectors collected more than what was due to fill their own pockets. Matthew did not think twice when Jesus said, "Follow me." These words to Matthew must have made their way straight to Matthew's heart. His heart probably was shocked by such compassion and loving acceptance. For a moment, he must have thought, "Me? I am just a tax collector. I can't change, I'm stuck here." Without a word, Matthew's heart said, "Yes! I'm yours!" There were no excuses, doubts or fears. His yes was his surrender to being loved.

What does God want when it comes to us? It is simple. He wants a loving relationship with His earthly children. He wants us. Love is absolutely the foundation of everything. God desires to be in our company. He has a deep affection for sinners. There is another reason why our Lord is interested in us. He purchased us with His own precious blood. Christ views the sinner, not as He is in Himself, but as He is in the purpose of Redemption. Jesus looks at us as to what He can make of us the sinner. He sees in every sinner the possibility of making a glorified saint who will dwell with Him forever. God sees us as we are.

Can we look up from our table today and see Jesus looking at us with compassion and love? I have felt His love and compassion. But sometimes I let the difficulties of the world overtake my heart. And that is when I feel so inadequate, a sinner who does not deserve God's love or grace. Do we meet His expectations? We never can do enough good. Why would God send His Son if being good enough would give us eternal life? By faith, Matthew followed Jesus. Nobody wanted Matthew, but Jesus wanted him.

Jesus knows and understands whatever has locked us into who we are here on this earth. Can we let ourselves experience and feel His love? Yes, turn from the world and turn to Jesus. His love is for all. And on the other side of that loving acceptance, there is freedom. Jesus is constantly asking us.

> *"As Jesus went on from there, He saw a man named Matthew sitting at the tax collector's booth. "Follow me," He told him, and Matthew got up and followed Him." (Matthew 9:9)*

> *"You mean, you want me."*

LOOK, WHAT I FOUND ALONG THE ROAD!

"For the word of God is alive and active. Sharper than any double-edged sword, it penetrates even to dividing soul and spirit, joints and marrow; it judges the thoughts and attitudes of the heart." (Hebrews 4:12)

et me tell you of a most wonderful experience that happened to me. God spoke to me as clearly as any words that have come into my mind. They were clear as if someone had said, "Good morning."

I was driving east out of town. There was an item lying in the middle of the roadway. It appeared to be a book. The pages were waving in the wind. A small voice said to me, "Turn around and see what this is on the road. It may be an important book, and maybe it is an old book." I love old books. As I moved along the road, the voice kept speaking, "Turn around, turn around." So, I listened to that small voice. I turned around and went back.

I pulled over to the side of the road, got out and picked it up. When I got in the car and looked at it, I knew it was an *important book*. It was the Bible! I looked through the Bible for any information that would tell me who the owner of this book might be. I only found a bookmark with these words, "God Bless our Home, Family, Friends & Country."

I wondered what God was up to when He told me to turn around and get this book. The effect this experience had on me was a fresh sense of God's reality. It strengthened my faith and secured the feeling that God is with me always. It is through the Bible that we can experience God speaking to us.

As food is necessary for growth and development in our physical life, so God's Word is necessary for the growth and maintenance of spiritual health. Because the Bible is God-breathed, it is different from any other book. The Bible is instruction for living from our God. It is His word of authority for our lives. Throughout its pages, we read, "Thus saith the Lord."

In 2 Timothy, Paul reminded Timothy of the importance of knowing the Word of God and using it as a guideline for life. In Chapter 3, Verse 16, Paul outlined for Timothy a four-fold way in which the Bible brings profit to life. It is profitable first, for doctrine; that is, for teaching. The Bible is useful to teach us what is true. Secondly, it is profitable for reproof, showing us where we are wrong, where we have deviated from God's plan. As we spend time in the Bible we realize what is wrong in our lives. Next, it is profitable for correction, setting and re-setting the direction of our lives in the right way. It straightens us out. It is also profitable for instruction in righteousness, how to keep us right and helps us do what is right. Keep us right with God.

There is a purpose for the Bible. The principles for everyday living and the answers to life's needs are in the Bible. Throughout my life, I have always had a Bible present. But have I opened it and read it throughout my life? I admit, I have not always made it a priority. We can find peace in His words if only we take the time to open it, read it and study it.

What has the Bible done for your life? for mine? Is it your Guidebook?

GOD'S WORD

"Your word is a lamp for my feet and a light for my path." (Psalm 119:105)

S cripture is not an obstacle. **Romans 15:4 assures us, "For** everything that was written in the past was written to teach us so that through the endurance taught in the Scriptures and the encouragement they provide we might have hope." We know the Bible was written by different people, different periods and we do believe it is God-breathed. All scripture is useful for teaching, for reproof, for correction and training in righteousness. We know God still speaks through it, not by us taking it literally. *Through us engaging and analyzing the Bible we will understand the context in which it was written.*

So how shall we read it? One answer is with head, heart and hands. Head to grapple with it, heart to love God through it, hands to obey what God says in it. The former Chief Rabbi, Jonathan Sacks, said, "The Bible isn't a book to be read and put down. It is God's invitation to join the conversation between heaven and earth."

As I grow in my faith, I do realize that scripture is especially important in growing my faith and growing my relationship with Jesus.

The Diary of a Bible (author unknown).

January 1- Family has made a New Year's resolution to read me every day. They read Matthew 1.

January 15- I have been resting quietly for a week. The first few nights, they read me regularly, but they have forgotten me.

February 11- The owner used me for a short time. He was asked to substitute for Bible class and had to look up some verses during breakfast. I went to Bible class but was put in the car between services. I have been in my owner's car for several weeks.

March 7- Spring cleaning going on. I was dusted and put back in an old place.

April 20- Grandma is here for a visit. I have been on her lap all afternoon. She spent most of her time on 1 Corinthians 13 and Chapter 15.

April 21, 22, 23- Read by Grandma every afternoon this week.

May 4- I have a few green stains on my pages, some early spring flowers pressed in me.

June 18- I look like a scrapbook. They have stuffed me full of clippings from the newspaper. One of the girls got married.

July 27- They packed me in a suitcase with clothes and other things. Off on vacation, I guess.

August 10- Still in a suitcase, though nearly everything else has been taken out.

August 14- Home again. Put me back in my old place. Quite a journey, though, I do not see why they wanted me to go along.

September 29- They used me once today. One of them is quite sick. Right now, I am shined up and on the center of the coffee table. I think the preacher is coming over.

October 19- Have lots of company and I am on the table. A comic book, TV Guide, Time magazine and a Movie World are on top of me. I wish I were read as much as they are.

November 11- Owner came home from worship services today, upset about something the preacher had said. Snatched me up to hunt for a verse but never found what he was looking for.

December 26- The family got a new TV set. The shelf I am on needed a bit more room, so they put me in a cabinet. I expect to get out around January 1ˢᵗ.

https://grandoldbook.com/diary_of_a_bible.pdf
Tell me, how would the 'Diary' of your Bible read?

A MATTER OF FAITH

"Now faith is confidence in what we hope for and assurance about what we do not see." (Hebrews 11:1)

"For we live by faith, not by sight." (2 Corinthians 5:7)

etting up on Sunday and going to church: do you think about why you do this? You probably do not think about it. You go to church by faith. You had faith your alarm clock would work, your car would start and the road would be passable. We exercise some faith every day of our lives. Our sleeping is faith. It takes faith in God to close our eyes and loosen our grip on the conscious world.

What is faith? Faith makes the things hoped for as real as if we already had them. Faith provides evidence that what is unseen is real. Faith is the confidence in the worthiness and ability of someone or something. Faith is setting your heart on the object of your hope and your confidence. There are inadequate objects of faith, such as money, security, wealth, other people and us. Put your focus on God. God is faith. Believe that He exists and that He rewards those who earnestly seek Him.

Faith is a matter of the heart. You may believe that God exists, but He may not be first in your life. Ask yourself, where is your hope, your faith right now? Who or what are you trusting today and for your future? Is it in yourself? Is it in your abilities? Is your life a testimony to faith in God? *Who has your heart today?*

"When Enoch had lived 65 years, he became the father of Methuselah. After he became the father of Methuselah, Enoch walked faithfully with God 300 years and had other sons and daughters. Altogether, Enoch lived a total of 365 years. Enoch walked faithfully with God; then he was no more because God took him away." (Genesis 5:21-24)

Enoch walked by faith in God. From Enoch we can learn that faith affects our walk and faith pleases God. Biblical faith is confidence in God, setting your heart on God. It is also knowing what has not yet happened is good and will be done by the will of God. Sometimes our faith is tested. "Remember how the LORD your God led you all the way in the wilderness these forty years, to humble and test you in order to know what was in your heart, whether or not you would keep his commands." (Deuteronomy 8:2) We need to know that the testing of our faith is going to happen. The Bible says "when" or "whenever," not IF. (John 16:33, Acts 14:22, 1 Peter 4:12) God has a reason and a purpose for the test of our faith.

God also uses these tests to work something through us. He wants to purify our hearts, teach us patience and to draw us closer to Him. Through this, God is helping us to become a mature and complete Christian. We need to check the pulse of our faith. Ask yourself, "Is it genuine?"

Through whatever trials God has for us through our life here on earth, we will ultimately be made to stand by God's power, and not our own. So, how big is your faith? We can all use some serious growth in our trust in God and His word. Take a good look in the Book of books and read it. Continue reading it until your faith starts shining bright and strong, no matter how dark the night.

Let us stand together and claim our FAITH IN GOD.

EMPOWERMENT OF JOY

"Though you have not seen Him, you love Him; and even though you do not see Him now, you believe in Him and are filled with an inexpressible and glorious joy, for you are receiving the end result of your faith, the salvation of your souls." 1 Peter 1:8-9

Through life, the majority of us including me, have gone through times of excitement, happiness and anticipation of good things. But along with this, we have times of sadness, disappointments and trials. Getting through these times is sometimes hard. We forget to take these to our Lord and lay them at His feet. This is when we find the peace, the strength and joy to go on. It is not easy to do because we want to control what is happening and fix it ourselves. But while we do, we do not find the joy in it. With our Lord in control, there will be joy even in difficult times.

The Lord calls us to be joyous people and have an abundant life. But how can we when our lives have disappointment, illness, death and difficulties? You might agree that it is hard to find many people who are full of joy. To understand the lifestyle God desires for us, we need to know the difference between joy and happiness. Both can be defined as gladness, delight and pleasure in something, but happiness has an external cause. When circumstances are favorable and delightful, we are naturally happy. When events take a downward turn, so do our spirits.

Joy is a feeling inside, not externally, as is happiness. As believers, we can keep our contentment in good times and bad. Our delight is in the Lord, not in our fluctuating circumstances. Since its source is our relationship with Christ, the joy the Bible describes is available only to Christians. Nehemiah said, "Go and enjoy choice food and sweet drinks, and send some to those who have nothing prepared. This day is holy to our Lord. Do not grieve, for the joy of the LORD is your strength." (Nehemiah 8:10) Joy is an empowering emotion that builds us up and gives us the ability to endure hardship. By choosing to rejoice when we do not feel like it, we will experience something inside of us. Shift your focus unto the Lord, delight in Him and remember all His blessings, even through difficult times.

Enjoy God. Christians are told to rejoice, not in the event that causes their suffering, but in the Lord. This is not a denial of our pain, but an opportunity to trust and praise God in it. Instead of focusing

on the situation, causing our misery, we should fix our eyes on Christ.
Then we will see the blessings that can cheer our hearts.

Only in God there is fullness of joy.
"The thief comes only to steal and kill and destroy. I came that
they may have life and have it abundantly." John 10:10

HOPE

"May the God of hope fill you with all joy and peace as you trust in him, so that you may overflow with hope by the power of the Holy Spirit." (Romans 15:13)

HOPE

May the God of hope fill you with all joy and peace
as you trust in him, so that you may overflow with hope
by the power of the Holy Spirit. — Romans 15:13

The dictionary definition of hope is to cherish a desire with anticipation, to want something to happen or be true. This hope is "a feeling we want to happen." Many times we say, "I hope we will have good weather." Or, "I hope I will win the lottery." This is not hoping. It is a feeling or wishful thinking. It is undependable and has no power to bring anything to pass.

Biblical hope is the anticipation of a favorable outcome under God's guidance. This hope is based on God's promises. In the Bible, hope is directive, active and life sustaining. Hope is a confident expectation. "For in this hope we were saved. But hope that is seen is no hope at all. Who hopes for what they already have? But if we hope for what we do not yet have, we wait for it patiently." (Romans 8:24-25) Biblical hope is never an escape from reality or from problems.

Hope often gets lost in our day to day struggles here in this world. The trials and difficulties of life have a way of eroding our hope. Often, they convince us that we are the only solution and we begin relying on our own abilities. The first mention of hope in Romans 15:13 refers to God as the origin of hope. The second time it is mentioned, we are the recipients of His hope. But no matter how difficult our circumstances, we can have hope because of who God is: powerful, wise, sovereign and good.

Remembering back through my younger years, my hopes were worldly hopes. I hope I get this job. I hope they choose me for the nomination. I hope my child can get on the team. And on they go. Perhaps you have had the same hopes. As we face life's trials and storms, what is it that we are hoping for? It is time to grab onto something that can carry us through tomorrow.

In whom do we place our hope: family, friends, material things, stock market? If it is in these, then that hope will end. Place your hope in God. Hope is like any virtue. It is God-given and can never die. We take it with us into eternity. Hope gives us energy and direction for our journey. Hope helps us keep our eyes on the finish line and cheers us on. Hope is an anchor to our soul. "God did this so that, by two unchangeable things in which it is impossible for God to lie, we who have fled to take hold of the hope set before us may be greatly encouraged. We have this hope as an anchor for the soul, firm and secure. It enters the inner sanctuary behind the curtain." (Hebrews 6:18-19)

Hope always remains a choice. We are called to live with open hands, to let go, so that something new can be given to us by God. Hope is not always a matter of only working for things outside of us to get better. That cannot always happen. Hope is also about improvement on the inside, becoming open to God to renew us, "Behold, I make all things new." (Revelation 21:5)

Has your hope grown dormant? Shift living in disappointment to living in hope and joy. Reawaken hope by asking God to forgive our dwelling on disappointments. Forgive those we have hurt. We also need to forgive ourselves for the poor choices we have made, and how we responded and coped in those circumstances. Be honest with God, with others and especially honest with ourselves. Ask God to renew your mind. "Do not conform to the pattern of this world, but be transformed by the renewing of your mind. Then you will be able to test and approve what God's will is—his good, pleasing and perfect will." (Romans 12:2)

I know what it is to be hopeless, to feel hopeless when life falls apart. I know what it is to watch those we love stumble through their days of hopelessness. My finding hope in God did not come overnight. It came slowly as my faith and trust grew. I learned to give my life circumstances over to God. I still have moments when I want to take hold and control the circumstances. I stop and pray and put the circumstances at the foot of the cross. It is only through my growth in faith and my relationship with Jesus that I have this hope that the Bible tells about. Faith is the beginning of hope. Believing is being grounded in faith. Ask yourself, "Am I rooted and centered in what matters? On what have I fixed my hope?" Remember always, God loves you, God will endure with you and God believes in you. Use your darkest days to encourage others to find hope and joy in their lives through Jesus Christ. As children of God, we have the hope and assurance that through the blood of Jesus Christ, the Son of God, we have eternal life.

Following, is a story of an old sailor at sea:

Finding an anchor for the storms of life.

The old sailor looked at the skies and saw a dark storm coming. As the sea became rough, the old salt calmly lowered the anchor link by link, battened down the hatches and went to bed for the night. He knew the storm would be rough. But he had faith in the grasp of the anchor. He knew his boat would be there in the morning.

Hope is our anchor. With faith we have an anchor. Scripture states that faith is the assurance of things hoped for.

https://www.gospelcrusader.com/hope-2/
"Let us hold unswervingly to the hope we profess, for He who promised is faithful." (Hebrews 10:23)

PATIENCE-UNDERSTANDING

"Trust in the Lord with all your heart and lean not on
your own understanding." (Proverbs 3:5)

O ne fall, I attended my granddaughter's 4-H horse show at their county fair. I was sitting alone in the bleacher section of the indoor arena, but soon other spectators joined me in the stands.

As we were all waiting patiently for the horse classes to start, the people around me were talking excessively. I am a person who appreciates quiet, so I was uneasy with all the racket. It seemed they knew each other. I felt uncomfortable as they encroached upon my personal space. I must admit, I began to think they were very rude and inconsiderate of others around them.

The 4-H classes started. At the beginning of one of the classes, the director of the 4-H club took the microphone and spoke. She spoke of a young girl who would be riding in the next class. She stated this was the first year this young girl participated in the 4-H equestrian events. She went on to tell us the young girl's story. A couple of years earlier, she was diagnosed with a brain tumor and she has gone through two major surgeries, as well as much rehabilitation. As she regained strength, she began riding her horse. Recently, they found the tumor had grown back and she would have her third surgery in a couple of weeks. The director spoke of the girl's determination and courage. The director announced she would be riding alone. The rest of the class would come in and join her.

As class started, the young girl came into the arena with her horse and did a short performance. The rest of the class entered the arena. The people around me had quieted down. I also noted tears in many of their eyes. I realized the people around me were this girl's family and friends. I felt sick, absolutely disgusted with myself for my thoughts and actions before her performance. Suddenly, everything changed. I changed.

Patience replaced impatience. Why? Because patience always hitches a ride with understanding. I had no idea these people were here supporting this young lady and her accomplishments. I saw a loud, annoying group of individuals with no consideration for those around them. Not until the truer picture unfolded did I understand their excitement. Without the broader view of what was to come, I was critical. And I judged them.

From this time on I ask God, "Am I seeing the whole picture or is there more to a situation than what I see?" I continue to pray for God to help me be more understanding and patient when I do not have a complete view of any circumstance. Without a larger view, we cannot understand. We cannot always see the big picture. God does. We should remember to ask ourselves, "Is there more to this situation?" and then be more patient. "Whoever derides their neighbor has no sense, but the one who has understanding holds their tongue." (Proverbs 11:12)

Before you blow up, listen up. Before you strike out, tune in.
"The impatient may not always be wrong on issues, but they are
almost always wrong in their attitudes." Quote by R. J. Rushdoony.

WILLING TO WAIT

"I remain confident of this: I will see the goodness of the LORD in the land of the living. Wait for the LORD; be strong and take heart and wait for the LORD." (Psalm 27:13-14)

Picture yourself waiting in any checkout line such as at the grocery store or drive-up banking that has not moved for ten minutes. Many of us would feel frustrated. We live in a generation that expects instant results.

Everyone struggles with some degree of impatience. We are born with this trait. The inborn reaction is to fuss at the first hint of discomfort and to keep at it until the need is met. For instance, when a baby is fussing, we consider the baby may be hungry, need a diaper changed or need a nap. Let us consider the biblical definition of patience. It can mean both longsuffering and perseverance, or not giving up and yielding under pressure. Patience means accepting what the Lord gives on His timetable, or what He chooses not to give. Being patient results in inner peace and a lack of stress. Meanwhile, we should pray, obey and persist as we seek God's direction.

The danger of impatience is that we might miss the Lord's perfect plan and His blessing. Only when we trust our Father's will and timing can we rest peacefully. As God's children, we are called to live a life worthy of Him. "Be completely humble and gentle; be patient, bearing with one another in love." (Ephesians 4:2) Scripture tells us to be tolerant of one another, bearing each other's burdens and responding with kindness, "Carry each other's burdens, and in this way you will fulfill the law of Christ." (Galatians 6:2) Our Lord is an example we should follow. He demonstrated patience toward Peter's hasty actions, the crowd's demands and the leaders' false accusations. We are to cultivate an attitude of composure. Our impatience can hurt others and close off dialogue. Calmly responding gives room for the other person to explain his attitude and make changes.

God offers us patience. Patience is a fruit of His Spirit. "But the fruit of the Spirit is love, joy, peace, forbearance (patience), kindness, goodness, faithfulness." (Galatians 5:22) Have you asked God to give you some fruit? If you did and you grew impatient, ask Him again and again and again. He will not grow impatient with your pleading. You will receive patience as you pray.

While you are praying, ask for understanding. "Whoever is patient has great understanding, but one who is quick-tempered displays folly." (Proverbs. 14:29) Why? Because patience always hitches a ride with understanding. The wise man says, "Whoever derides their neighbor has no sense, but the one who has understanding holds their tongue." (Proverbs 11:12) He also says, "The one who has knowledge uses words with restraint, and whoever has understanding is even-tempered." (Proverbs 17:27) Do not miss the connection between understanding and patience.

God is patient with you. And if God is patient with you, cannot you pass it on.

Wait Upon the Lord

As humans tend to be,
I want my solace now.
One hundred times today alone,
I have passed my load to you,
But then I pick it up again.
So, Lord, this time when I shift the load,
And you take it up for me,
Please help me wait with faith. Amen

TRUST GOD FOR RESTORATION

"Then He said to her, "Daughter, your faith has healed you. Go in peace." (Luke 8:48)

n Luke 8, there are two scenes where a girl was restored to life and a woman healed. A man named Jairus, a leader of the synagogue, came to Jesus pleading with Him to come to his house for his twelve-year-old daughter was dying. Also, as Jesus was traveling through the crowd, a woman who has been suffering from a hemorrhage for twelve years came up behind Jesus and touched the hem of His garment. Immediately she was healed.

The woman and this young daughter had a planned health detour. Some health detours take us from good health and end in a long illness and may end in death. In Psalm 139:13-24, we see that God has a specific design for each of us. The young girl's health detour ended in death, but through God's sovereignty, she came back to life. Let us call this a God Thing One, first-class miracle. God suspended natural law. Jairus heard these words, "Only believe, and she will be well." The woman was healed immediately, let us call this a God Thing Two. This is a second-class miracle. It can be called a "come back." The woman heard these words, "Your faith has made you well."

God is a planner. From beginning to end, He plans our lives. God did not look away and then you got sick. It was a planned event. We go through life and then an event happens. For example, we get pneumonia. This is a natural event that happens from our good health. Colds and flu are normal and expected, but you usually bounce back to good health. Some deviations from this do not seem normal, such as cancer, heart disease, car accident and a slow decline in health.

In my last health detour planned by God, I went from good health to bad health. I glorify Him and sing praises to Him for His miracle in my life. God healed me through my faith and trust in Him. God gave me confidence and reassured me that I would be okay no matter what. I had a comeback! I remember offering a short breath prayer to God when the ambulance brought me to the ER. My prayer was, "Daddy (Father), you are in control in this situation. I cannot control it, the doctors and nurses cannot control it, no one can but you. I will accept whatever outcome you have for me and will continue my life for you in any situation. I love you. I pray this day in the name of Jesus

Christ, Amen." As opportunity presents itself after the stroke and going forward, I will glorify God for my wondrous recovery. I will make it known and glorify Him.

It is not always easy to give God our lives in situations that test our faith and trust. I am not saying it comes easy for me. It does not. Throughout my life, as with everyone, our life has many health detours and other detours. If we can give these situations to God and let Him handle it, we will find ourselves in His will. Let us let Him be God.

Christ is compassionate: God cares about our
pain and suffering and has compassion.
Christ is omnipotent, powerful: God holds together the universe,
so why would not He be all-powerful with our bodies.
God is sovereign: God can do all things and accomplish all things.
He determines what happens in our life, in America and the world.

JESUS REMEMBER ME

"Then he said, "Jesus, remember me when you come into your kingdom. Jesus answered him, "Truly I tell you, today you will be with me in paradise." (Luke 23:42-43)

"As they were walking along the road, a man said to Him, "I will follow you wherever you go." (Luke 9:57)

There were two criminals on Calvary with Jesus to be put to death. One was on the right side of Jesus and the other on the left side of Jesus. "One of the criminals who hung their hurled insults at Him. "Aren't you the Messiah? Save yourself and us." (Luke 23:39) This criminal on the left joined the taunting mob. But the repentant thief on the right, aware that he was dying and had nothing to fear, spoke in Jesus' defense. "But the other criminal rebuked him. "Don't you fear God," he said, "since you are under the same sentence? We are punished justly, for we are getting what our deeds deserve. But this man has done nothing wrong." (Luke 23:40-41)

Both thieves wanted to be saved. However, the thief on the Lord's left did not have saving faith. He said, "If thou be the Christ…" Like much of the world, the thief on the left wanted salvation from the penalty of sin, but not from sin itself. He lacked saving faith. Jesus says, "I told you that you would die in your sins; if you do not believe that I am He, you will indeed die in your sins." (John 8:24) The keyword here is if. Without faith, it is impossible to please God (Hebrews 11:6). Also, when Jesus was tempted in the wilderness, the devil said, "If thou be the Son of God." (Matthew 4:3)

Even though Jesus was suffering on the cross, He never failed to hear a sincere cry for help. In answer to the thief's plea, "Lord, remember me." "Jesus answered him, "Truly I tell you, today you will be with me in paradise." (Luke 23:43) These must be the greatest words ever spoken.

The difference between the criminals was only one of them asked to be a part of Jesus' kingdom. One asked to be saved but the other did not. One had faith in Jesus but the other did not. The one who asked knew he needed Jesus and was not proud to ask. And because he asked for grace, Jesus offered it and promised it.

A lesson we learn from the saved thief is we are all sinners in need of a Savior. It is never too late to repent, no matter the number of sins or we think our sins are minor or extreme. And so, we are left with a question: Have we recognized deep in our hearts our need for Jesus Christ? Have we acknowledged we are utterly lost without Him? Stop and seek deep into your heart for the answers. Ask Jesus for His grace, mercy and forgiveness.

We should remember Jesus took on our diseases. He heals us in mind, body and spirit. Remember salvation is for the whole person.

The following story illustrates this point.

> Officer Peter O'Hanlon was patrolling on night duty in northern England some years ago when he heard a quivering sob. Turning, he saw in the shadows a little boy sitting on a doorstep. With tears rolling down his cheeks, the child whimpered, "I'm lost. Please take me home." Where do you live, child? What street?" the officer asked. "I don't know," the little boy whimpered.
>
> The policeman began naming street after street, trying to help the young boy remember where he lived. When that failed, he repeated the names of the shops and hotels in the area, but all without success. Then, he remembered that in the center of the city was a well-known church with a large white cross that rose high above the surrounding landscape. He pointed to it and asked, "Do you live anywhere near that?" The boy's face immediately brightened. "Yes sir, take me to the cross. I can find my way home from there!"

https://sermons.faithlife.com/
sermons/92575-disciples-response-to-the-cross

We will never find the way to our heavenly home unless we begin our journey at the foot of the cross.

Salvation is for today – not for tomorrow.

Hope is for today – not for tomorrow.

A new beginning with God is for today – not for tomorrow.

Jesus is for today. And Jesus says the same thing to each one of us:

"Today, you will be with me in Paradise."

Have you made your decision to take up your cross and follow Jesus?

ONE PAIR OF HANDS

"You shall be a crown of beauty in the hand of the Lord, and a royal diadem in the hand of your God." (Isaiah 6:3)

The Bible speaks of God having hands. God's fearful hands, saving hands, keeping hands, helping hands and strong hands. God's hands created the mountains, the seas and every living thing on earth.

Jesus' hands were scarred as they nailed Him to the cross. In Heaven, we will not be scarred. Jesus' hands will bear the only scars in Heaven. "Can a mother forget the baby at her breast and have no compassion on the child she has borne? Though she may forget, I will not forget you! See, I have engraved you on the palms of my hands; your walls are ever before me." (Isaiah 49:15-16) There are times when we feel that God is not close, that He has abandoned us. Remember, His scarred hands are holding us eternally secure. "I give them eternal life, and they shall never perish; no one will snatch them out of my hand. My Father, who has given them to me, is greater than all, no one can snatch them out of my Father's hand." (John 10:28-29)

I am sure you have reached out your hands to your children. Let us say they want to jump into the pool or the lake. They stand there, asking, "Will you catch me?" We say, "Yes, trust me, I am right here." They jump in and we catch them, and now they want to do it repeatedly. Other times we take their hands in a strange place, while crossing a street or in any situation when our help is needed. God also takes our hands and helps us travel into the unknown and fearful events of our lives. Remember this scripture verse. "When I am afraid, I put my trust in you." (Psalm 56:3)

We must put our faith into God's hands. As Mother Teresa put it, we will need sharpening as we go along. My faith wavers at times, but as I bring myself to prayer and leave it in God's hands, I am assured of His love, peace, strength and comfort. This is what gives me the strength to persevere. As our faith waivers as life circumstances come to us, remember our lives are in His hands.

Nothing can shake those who are secure in God's hands.

LIFE ON THE OUTSIDE

"So do not fear, for I am with you; do not be dismayed, for I am your God. I will strengthen you and help you; I will uphold you with my righteous right hand." (Isaiah 41:10)

"Be strong and courageous. Do not be afraid or terrified because of them, for the LORD your God goes with you; he will never leave you nor forsake you." Deuteronomy 31:6

"Turn to me and be gracious to me, for I am lonely and afflicted." (Psalm 25:16)

E veryone struggles with loneliness at some point, when you are going through something hard or having a change in life. You may not think anyone else understands. You just feel alone. God's word provides hope and strength.

In February 2002, I discovered what real loneliness was. You see, my husband of over 35 years died. On that day, I felt as though I had also died. Here I was, still alive. There was a huge void in my life. Loneliness has been part of my whole life. It keeps popping up now and then. When we are lonely, we want it to go away, but too often we find it keeps coming back. We can feel alone even when we are with family or friends. It is painful. At that moment, you feel as if it is just you. We can find it easy just to isolate ourselves from others. The isolation triggers can be our stages in life: adolescent, adulthood, launching our children, empty nest. There are moments in our lives when a transition has taken place. A change in schools, a move, loss of health and loss of loved ones. We can be misunderstood and labeled by our faith, values, hobbies, etc. Our life has challenges, raising a special need child, a disabled spouse, our own health issues and other life happenings.

Triggers push us into isolation. Sometimes we step back and isolate ourselves. We feel like no one cares, no one gets me, no one loves me. We feel like that in certain groups. We feel like an island and it consumes our day. We are good at hiding it, but when we hide it, it only gets worse.

What does God say about loneliness? God created us and our emotions. He surely understands us. And Jesus experienced loneliness. On the cross Jesus felt forsaken by His Father. And His most committed disciples forsook Him at His greatest hour of need. Jesus Christ has experienced every human emotion. He knows what it is like to be lonely.

David also felt loneliness. In a series of earnest, heartfelt appeals to God, David cried out in his loneliness and despair. His son Absalom rose against him, the men of Israel went after him, and he was forced to flee from the city. He left his house and family feeling lonely and afflicted. "So do not fear, for I am with you; do not be dismayed, for I am your God. I will strengthen you and help you; I will uphold you with my righteous right hand." (Isaiah 41:10) David's only recourse was to turn to God and plead for mercy and God's intervention. His only hope was in God.

There are three basic causes of loneliness. (excerpt from Bible. org). 1) *Separation from God* - God created us to live in fellowship with Him, but sin broke that fellowship. God sent His son to restore our relationship with Him. Through Jesus' death and our fellowship with Christ, we have been restored with God. We may be lonely for people, friends, a mate, but if we trust in the Lord Jesus, we never have to be lonely for God again. We have His assurance that He is always with us and in us. We need to build our fellowship with God. We can do this by spending quiet time with Him even if it is 15 minutes a day, read scripture and by practicing the presence of God.

2) *Separation from people* – God has built in us a desire to be with others. Robin Williams once stated, "I used to think that the worst thing in life was to end up alone. It is not. The worst thing in life is to end up with people who make you feel alone." God created us to have relationships with other people. There are some steps we can take. Reach out to others. Take the phone and call a friend instead of waiting for the phone to ring. Some suggestions are lunch or an outing together. Reach out to God. Join a Bible study group. Think about volunteering and reach out to others on the outside.

3) *Separation from ourselves* – Sometimes our feelings of loneliness indicate a sense of alienation from ourselves. If we are honest with ourselves, we will admit there are things in our own personalities we do not like. There are times when things seem to be going wrong, and we feel frustrated and discouraged. When we dwell on our failures and our shortcomings, we generate our loneliness. When this happens, remember that God loves us. Then receive His love. Accept God's evaluation of us, and we will not be controlled by our feelings of inadequacy and loneliness. Have confidence in His ability to make us the person He wants us to be. We will then be free and controlled

by His Holy Spirit. When you know you are loved, it changes the way you feel about yourself.

https://bible.org/seriespage/lesson-17-lessons-loneliness

The "Winter Season" of life can be a season of loneliness. In this season, you are retired. The loss of a spouse may present retirement in a whole different way. Children have their own lives and grandchildren are off to college and beginning their lives. Our bodies starts to fail and it is harder to do normal activities. You may feel isolated from your family. We are not as involved in the work community and it is hard to feel useful.

When we look to others to fulfill our need and comfort our hurt, we are bound to be disappointed and loneliness sets in. I found myself in this lonely season. But the most wonderful thing is that our Almighty God is with us in this loneliness. We are never alone, never apart from His love. Have you ever thought that maybe God placed you in this lonely time for a reason? We are so busy, we often leave little time for God. When we are alone, God has the opportunity to speak to us. Nine times in the gospels, we are told that Jesus went away to a lonely place to be with the Father. Jesus sought out solitude so he could seek the Father's will for His life.

One day I went for a walk. We had a park nearby and I often went there to sit on a bench and take in the sights and sounds. As I watched a bird sitting alone on a wire, I thought about a passage I read in the Psalms. "I am like a desert owl, like an owl among the ruins. I lie awake; I have become like a bird alone on a roof." (Psalm 102:6-7) The psalmist who wrote about the owl said, "Why, my soul, are you downcast? Why so disturbed within me? Put your hope in God, for I will yet praise Him, my Savior, and my God." (Psalm 42:5) Reach out to the cross and say, "Lord, I open my heart and my life to You. I commit myself to You."

Instead of running from loneliness, allow God
to use it to draw you closer to Him.

QUIT COMPARING

"We do not dare to classify or compare ourselves with some who commend themselves. When they measure themselves by themselves and compare themselves with themselves, they are not wise." (2 Corinthians 10:12)

I **n nature, we can compare eagles to robins to pigeons. While** they are all considered birds, they are not the same. There is also a value to comparing, box to another box, coupon to another coupon, animal to another animal. Comparing can help our strengths and help us to know our weaknesses.

Why do we compare? Why do we compare ourselves to others' looks, intelligence, career or spouse. Perhaps we compare to be more accepted and loved. Our pride and ego take us to a bad place.

Biblically we can learn from:

Cain and Abel (Genesis 4:1-7)- Cain and Abel were different. Abel, by faith, brought some of his fat portions of the first-born of the flock. Cain brought some of the fruits of the soil as an offering. God did not compare Abel to Cain's offering. Cain was holding back and did not have a spirit of joy but of obligation. *Do what is right.*

Esau and Jacob (Genesis 25:19-34)- Twins Esau and Jacob struggled in their mother's womb, and it continued throughout their relationship. Esau was a hunter, a man of the field, while Jacob was quiet and tended the crops. Esau was to get the blessing from Isaac because he was the oldest.

One day Jacob had prepared a stew, and because Esau was famished, Jacob asked for his birthright. He took advantage of Esau. Esau said, "Because I am about to die; of what use is a birthright to me?" *We cannot be equal, but we can be fair.*

Saul and David (1 Samuel 18:5-30)- Saul was always comparing himself with David. He was angry and jealous of David. Why? Saul had a big ego problem. Saul knew he did not have the spiritualty compared to David. Saul also knew he was sinning and was afraid of David. *When comparison gets into our soul, it hurts us.*

John the Baptist and Jesus- John was the forerunner before Jesus. There are similarities between John and Jesus. Both John and Jesus were conceived in miraculous circumstances. The angel Gabriel visited Zachariah and announced Elizabeth would bear a son in her old age. Gabriel also visited Mary and announced she would bear a son conceived of the Holy Spirit. John and Jesus both received authority from heaven. John preached repentance and the coming of the Messiah. John acknowledged Jesus as the Son of God. Jesus must increase and I must decrease. "But these are written that you may believe that Jesus is the Messiah, the Son of God, and that by believing you may have life in His name." (John 20:31)

We should elaborate our God-given gifts and our design. Our heavenly Father gives us spiritual gifts. "All these are the work of one and the same Spirit, and he distributes them to each one, just as he determines." (1 Corinthians 12:11) Everybody gets a gift, nobody goes without.

We all are specially designed. We are called to live the life we are given. Each one of us has unique value, insight and experience God wants to work through. Our lives were not meant to be a comparison party where we continually attempt to gain or achieve other people's stuff and circumstances. When we are who God made us to be, people can look at our lives and ask, "How does he/she have so much peace amid _____?" or "How can he/she be so generous when he/she has so little?"

God operates by grace. Stop comparing and live by grace.

> *Matthew 20:8-16: "When evening came, the owner of the vineyard said to his foreman, 'Call the workers and pay them their wages, beginning with the last ones hired and going on to the first.' "The workers who were hired about five in the afternoon came and each received a denarius. So, when those came who were hired first, they expected to receive more. But each one of them also received a denarius. When they received it, they began to grumble against the landowner. 'These who were hired last worked only one hour,' they said, 'and you have made them equal to us who have borne the burden of the work and the heat of the day.' "But he answered one*

of them, 'I am not being unfair to you, friend. Didn't you agree to work for a denarius? Take your pay and go. I want to give the one who was hired last the same as I gave you. Don't I have the right to do what I want with my own money? Or are you envious because I am generous?'
"So, the last will be first, and the first will be last."

LET GOD PUT YOUR PIECES TOGETHER

"The Lord works out everything to its proper end—
even the wicked for a day of disaster." (Proverbs 16:4)

"For I know the plans I have for you," declares the
Lord, "plans to prosper you and not to harm you, plans
to give you hope and a future." (Jeremiah 29:11)

M y granddaughters and I started a puzzle in the library room where I was living at the time. We had a great start. We did the corners and the outer edges of the puzzle. Each time we worked on it, we made progress on the 1,000-piece puzzle. It is not a quick project. After coming back from a two-week vacation, I went to the library to work on it one evening. To my surprise, the puzzle was taken apart, put in a bag and put in the corner. Someone had started their puzzle where ours was. I was very disheartened. I needed to explain what happened to the girls and pondered how to explain it to them. My first instinct was from Satan himself, "Break theirs apart and start yours again." I thought, "This is not a thought from God." God would not ask me to do this. I returned to my apartment. Several days went by and it was still on my mind. I thought, "What would Jesus do?" He would put the pieces together again, just like He puts our pieces of life together. He holds the pieces to make us whole again.

I would imagine that we all have worked on a puzzle sometime in our life. We have learned to appreciate the picture on the cover of the box. I usually prop up the box cover and begin looking for colors, designs and lines that help sort out the pieces. Without the picture, I would be lost trying to figure out the puzzle.

Our lives are a lot like a puzzle. The only difference is that we do not have a drawing to guide us as we put our lives together. Our lives progress piece by piece. I have had so many pieces of my life either lost or broken. They just did not fit or I had difficulty putting things back together. But I found out that on my own, I have limited knowledge and strength to fit my life back together. It becomes overwhelming for me.

Most of us start with the corner pieces to frame our puzzle, as they are obvious to us. There are those things we know that frame or anchor our lives, and we know where to put them. We slowly get brave and begin to put the edge pieces of our lives together. Then we, without much planning, begin haphazardly filling in the middle of our puzzle. Each of us has a puzzle to put together. Others can help place our pieces. But we alone can determine if the piece fits.

Our puzzle can spill off the table or be knocked about, and the pieces are jumbled up. This happens through carelessness or neglect, either on our part or someone else's. We are left to pick up the pieces, place them back in the box and start over. Each time our puzzle jumbles, we learn to put the pieces back together carefully.

It is impossible to force the pieces to fit. If you try to force the pieces, the edges of the puzzle will either separate or crease and damage the puzzle. This is what happens to our life when we want to do what we want to do and not walk in God's will for us. God knows what the picture looks like and guides us to the things that will allow us to be that picture. God fits each piece of the puzzle together perfectly.

God has a plan for us. We need to remember to talk to Him and follow His ways. He knows what the picture looks like. He made the blueprint. Our framework for our entire lives should be determined by the Word of God. It is not always going to be easy to put the middle sections of the puzzle together in our lives. I daily go about placing pieces of my life in place, failing to ask God what His will is for me. We need to remember to come to Him and ask for His will.

"By the grace God has given me, I laid a foundation as a wise builder, and someone else is building on it. But each one should build with care. For no one can lay any foundation other than the one already laid, which is Jesus Christ. If anyone builds on this foundation using gold, silver, costly stones, wood, hay or straw, their work will be shown for what it is, because the Day will bring it to light. It will be revealed with fire, and the fire will test the quality of each person's work. If what has been built survives, the builder will receive a reward. If it is burned up, the builder will suffer loss but yet will be saved—even though only as one escaping through the flames." (1 Corinthians 3:9-15)

I will continue to build my life puzzle with faith and trust in my Lord. I know that God has all the pieces I need, whether they are painful pieces or pieces of beauty. For we are co-workers in God's service. You are God's field, God's building.

What does your life puzzle look like?

LIFE'S DISAPPOINTMENTS

Dear Jesus,
I tried so hard to make it work but I failed. This
situation did not end the way that I had hoped and
expected it would. I am so disappointed.
I sought Your will and I thought I knew what to do. I used great
care, moving forward toward the goal, and I often stopped to pray.
Your Child.

*https://www.faithgateway.com/disappointment-
jesus-tried-hard/#.X8AzOM1KjIU*

nyone can write this letter. One time a situation presented itself and it was devastating to my daughter's family and me. For five years, we did everything that was expected of us only to have it all fall apart. I prayed often and put my faith in God. I asked Him to show us a purpose for what we were going through, and what good would come from this catastrophe. In my prayers I continued to tell God that we would accept whatever outcome He has for us, for it will be His will, not ours.

When it all fell apart and there was no resolve, we were left with nothing but pain, heartache and disappointment. I asked God, "Why didn't you intervene? God, why have we had to go through this? God, why do you seem so far away, so hidden, so silent?" I felt disappointed that God was so quiet. Shouldn't He be more attentive in our need?

Read Mark 5:21-43. Our struggles with Jesus' silence may reveal something about us. Is our faith in our Lord or the struggle? Where are our eyes going to be? Where is our heart going to be? God does promise to help in our time of need. "Come to me, all you who are weary and burdened, and I will give you rest." (Matthew 11:28)

God waits until the best time to act. "There is a time for everything and a season for every activity under the heavens." (Ecclesiastes 3:1) His timing is right. We may never know why. God promises absolute and complete deliverance through FAITH in Jesus Christ. "Look, I am coming soon! My reward is with me, and I will give to each person according to what they have done." (Revelation 22:12)

Read Mark 5:21-43. Four thoughts from this scripture. *Sermon from Pastor P. Wagner, Trinity Lutheran Church, Waconia, MN*

1. Our struggles with Jesus' silence may reveal something about us. Is your faith in our Lord or the struggle? Where are your eyes going to be? Where is your heart going to be?
2. God does promise to help in our time of need. "Come to me, all you who are weary and burdened, and I will give you rest." (Matthew 11:28)

3. God waits until the best time to act. "There is a time for everything, and a season for every activity under the heavens." (Ecclesiastes 3:1) We may never know, but His timing is right.

4. God promises absolute and complete deliverance through *Faith* in Jesus Christ. "See, Look, I am coming soon! My reward is with me, and I will give to each person according to what they have done." (Revelation 22:12)

It is not wrong to feel disappointed with God, but the enemy would have you believe God is not listening to you and He does not care about you. We need to remind ourselves of God's great love for us.

I accepted the outcome knowing God answered my prayers even though the result was not at all what we hoped for. Although we had feelings of abandonment by God, as time passed, we realized God did not abandon us nor His plans for our lives. We do not always understand the ways of God and His purposes. "For my thoughts are not your thoughts, neither are your ways my ways," declares the Lord. "As the heavens are higher than the earth, so are my ways higher than your ways and my thoughts than your thoughts." (Isaiah 55: 8-9) After many years had passed, one day it came to me there was something good that came out of our struggle. "And we know that in all things God works for the good of those who love Him, who have been called according to His purpose." (Romans 8:28)

It is important we keep our perspective and look forward to eternity. It is when we are disappointed with God our faith is most tested. It is then we choose to believe His goodness and wait on His faithfulness. "Wait for the Lord; be strong and take heart and wait for the Lord." (Psalm 27:14)

"I have fought the good fight, I have finished
the race, I have kept the faith."
(2 Timothy 4:7)
God is Faithful Yesterday, Today, & Tomorrow.
Remember the absolute sovereignty of God.

AN UNEXPECTED GIFT

"Every good and perfect gift is from above, coming down from the Father of heavenly lights, who does not change like shifting shadows." (James 1:17)

The year my husband died I took the regular trip that we always did to the Lake Superior North Shore on fishing opener weekend in May. It was a journey I needed to take. I wanted to do all the things that my husband and I did year after year. The first stop was always at an antique store. It was a unique store. Both of us enjoyed their collection of old books.

I stopped and went in to look at their old books. I found a book written by Henri Nouwen and went to the counter to pay. The owner was easy to talk to. He asked where I was from and where I was going. I told him about my journey and how this journey was hard but necessary for me to do. He listened with a kind and empathetic ear. As I was leaving, he came around from the counter and asked if he could give me a hug.

Before I stopped at the shop, I was contemplating turning around and going back home. I was thinking, "This trip is too hard." But as I returned to the car from the shop, I felt a new and fresh feeling about this trip and headed out to continue my journey. As I was driving, I realized that God was touching me through the owner's kind words and his hug. What had just happened gave me the strength to go on. I completed the journey that weekend and enjoyed tracing the steps my husband and I always did.

The next year I again went up to the North Shore and stopped at the antique shop. This time the wife of the owner was there. I looked around the shop and picked up a book to purchase. After paying for the book, I asked if her husband told her about a lady who stopped by last year on a journey of remembrance. She said that he had not. There were no other customers in the store, so I told her the story. I asked her to tell her husband that he was my gift from God that weekend. That through her husband's words and the hug, I found the courage to continue my journey. He had no idea how his hug and kindness impacted and changed the situation for me that day. Now, every time I go to the North Shore, I stop at the shop and get my hug.

Often God speaks through our quiet moments, through other people and life's circumstances. God positively spoke to me through the owner of the shop. People can deny Christ, dispute Scripture and ignore prophecy, but they cannot deny, dispute, or ignore God's power in someone's life. Our stories of pain, adversity, joy and His interaction in our life are meant to serve as a testimony of God's faithfulness and power. I have since learned it is always God's desire for us to share our stories. God never wastes our pain. Only we do that.

Lord, help me find the courage and the desire to share what
You have done in my life. Turn my past into my purpose and
refuse to let my pain be for nothing. In Jesus' name, Amen.

AN ODD COUPLE

"I pray that your partnership with us in the faith may be effective in deepening your understanding of every good thing we share for the sake of Christ." (Philemon 1:6)

O pen your Bible and read John 4:7-26. It tells of Jesus meeting a woman at the well who was shunned by her community. These scripture verses also show a great deal about Jesus' character. It is an excellent example of how Jesus shared His faith. Notice that Jesus spoke to the woman at the well when she was alone. We will often find people are more open, honest and receptive when they are alone. To share your faith, all you need is a bit of knowledge, humility and kindness.

I took my car in for an oil change. The manager was alone in the office. He took my information and brought my car into the garage. The manager returned and went about his business. All of a sudden he started a conversation with me. He talked about what was troubling him. He said he had just broken up with his girlfriend and it was mutual between them. But it was still hard, and he was trying to adjust to being alone without her. I thought, "Why is this young man opening up to me on what was troubling him?"

He mentioned he wanted to take this time to be a better man and to enjoy being alone and not always feeling like he needed someone. Also, he mentioned starting a Men's Bible Study group. I acknowledged this was a good step for him to take.

He continued to share how he was feeling and how his mind would not be quiet. This young man was anxious and worried. I had experienced those same feelings. I shared my story and what I learned from them. I told him to read Philippians 4:6-7, "Do not be anxious about anything, but in every situation, by prayer and petition, with thanksgiving, present your requests to God. And the peace of God, which transcends all understanding, will guard your hearts and your minds in Christ." I asked him why he does not give this situation to God? God does not want us to be anxious about anything. "Trust in the LORD with all your heart and lean not on your own understanding." (Proverbs 3:5) We continued with his questions and concerns, and I shared my life experiences and my growth in faith and trust in God.

Our conversation was interrupted now and then, but when we were alone, the young man went right back to where our conversation left off. We continued sharing our faith in God and our lives for an hour. Then my car was done. While I was paying my bill, he said, "Sandy, thank you so very much for this time together." He then pointed upward and said, "I need to thank God also." I said, "Yes, in this today may God be glorified."

Going into that day, I never thought that I would be engaged in a faith conversation with a young man, sharing my experiences and sharing my relationship with Jesus. When I drove home, I thought what an odd couple - a 27-year-old young man and a 72-year-old lady. I knew that God had connected us.

Having a spiritual conversation is an insurmountable task. Sometimes the biggest hurdle is just getting started. In the past, sharing the Gospel often meant focusing on encouraging people to give their lives to Christ.

These days few people have even a basic grasp of Jesus' story. Sometimes we want to engage in conversation in hopes of an opportunity to share the Gospel. Sometimes the conversation happens intentionally, with a question or is completely spontaneous like the conversation I had with the young man at the auto repair shop.

I think what makes spiritual conversations difficult is that we are not always sure what we are going to say and we are not always sure how the other person is going to react. However, you can be sure that God wants to use you to influence other people.

Take a step of faith. Ask God to use you to help someone move closer to Jesus. It is a good idea to listen more than you talk. Allow the other person the freedom to express their feelings. The moment you begin to tell them how they should feel is the moment the conversation will stop. Listen for opportunities to share your story and realize that your life is an example to others.

Always have complete confidence and trust in the Holy Spirit.
"Our faith becomes stronger as we express it; a growing
faith is a sharing faith." — Billy Graham

AN UNLIKELY PLACE I FOUND GOD

"You will seek me and find me when you seek me with all your heart." (Jeremiah 29:13)

"Blessed are the pure in heart, for they will see God." (Matthew 5:8)

Elijah searched for God in a whirlwind but found Him in a whisper. Jacob found Him in his dreams. Moses found Him in a burning bush. Mary Magdalene looked for Him in a tomb but found Him standing behind her. God seems to turn up in unexpected places. God is a God of surprises. He visits us incognito.

In Genesis 28:17 Jacob is traveling across a foreign land at his father Isaac's command. Esau, his brother, deceived Isaac and was threatening Jacob. On this journey God gave Jacob a dream. Jacob went from being unaware of God's presence to being aware of God's presence. This was life changing. Jacob can surely say that the presence of the Lord was in his place. We can also say that it is awesome as we experience God's presence in our own lives. We know we had an experience with the presence of God, in that moment and in that place. All we can say is that the presence of the Lord is in this place and it is holy.

My cousin was a young man at the time he died. He lived in Colorado, but his family brought him back to Minnesota for a memorial and burial service. The service was going to be held in his hometown. The family chose a local bar establishment instead of his home church. I was surprised, but then again, I was not. My cousin was more comfortable at a bar and driving his Harley than probably anywhere else.

The establishment had closed off part of the bar to hold the service. While sitting there waiting for the service to begin we could hear the voices and noise from the individuals in the bar. I wondered who would be officiating the service and what music would be played. It was not that I was uncomfortable, but I would say a little uneasy about being in a bar for a memorial service. Everyone was noticeably quiet. I was wondering if others attending are having the same thoughts I was.

A lady playing a keyboard started the service with music. The pastor came forward and introduced himself as the current pastor of the home church of my cousin. He did not offer any explanation of why we are here at the bar and not at the church. The program of the service was no different than any other memorial service. Hymns,

Bible Scripture, readings, Pastor's message and the obituary. Then my cousin's wife spoke. She also did not offer any information as to why the service was held at the bar. She spoke of his life, family and his loves.

As the service went on, I could feel peace, love and the presence of our Lord. God was there in our singing, prayers and the message we received. I thought how the walls of this place and the bar noise in the background, made no difference to God. I could not have felt God any closer than if I had been in church.

God's presence feels different to different people, and even in different ways in different circumstances. It goes way beyond the description of feeling. At the heart of it, it is a simply knowing that something greater than us is making His presence known in the room. It can be accompanied by events, a simple inner knowing or what other people are sensing at the same moment you are.

For me, the memorial service was a powerful sense of connection with Him. It added a lightness to the room that was more spiritual than physical. It manifested itself in the hymns we sang. The calmer I became, the more I sensed His presence. I noticed throughout my years that when I am without expectation and I just simply seek His presence, I feel His presence.

After my husband died, I met with my Stephen Minister once a week at our favorite restaurant. One week we met, ordered our meal, shared our week events and prayed. As we were praying, I could feel the presence of Jesus. I had a vision of Jesus standing at the end of the booth with His arms raised and a hand over each of our heads. He was there until we finished praying. I told my Stephen Minister about my vision as we prayed, and she verified it by telling me she felt like we were in a bubble. Well, we were in a bubble of sorts. We were encased in Jesus' arms. For many of us, it is not that God is not making Himself known, it is that we have not yet tuned ourselves in to Him.

It is a blessing to recognize His voice and feel His presence. We need to belong to Him for us to feel or hear Him. "My sheep listen to my voice; I know them, and they follow me." (John 10:17) God speaks to us through His Word. He will never lead us in any way that contradicts His word. You will feel a great sense of peace.

God is omnipresent, meaning He is always present in all places. Having the reality of God's presence is not dependent on our being in a particular circumstance or place. It is only dependent on our determination to keep the Lord before us continually.

God is present, just talk to Him.

ENTERTAIN STRANGERS

"Do not forget to show hospitality to strangers, for by so doing some people have shown hospitality to angels without knowing it." (Hebrews 13:2)

ENTERTAIN STRANGERS

Do not forget to show hospitality to strangers, for by so doing some people have entertained angels without knowing it. (Hebrews 13:2)

was looking after two of my granddaughters for seven days while their mother went on vacation. Early one evening, we went to the airport to pick her up. I wanted to get to the airport an hour earlier, so we would not be rushed. We could go inside, grab a bite to eat, relax and wait.

Once at the airport, we picked out some items to eat, and after eating, we went to the baggage claim area. There were four seats in a row, and three were empty with a young man sitting in the end seat. I sat down next to him and the girls sat next to me. In just a short time, my granddaughter JD, eight years old at the time, was up and prancing around. She wanted her sissy TKB, sixteen years old, to provide rap music for her. TKB went right ahead, making rap rhythms with her mouth. After a few minutes, the young man said to JD, "You like rap?"

She said, "Yes."

He began to get his iPod out and said, "I have a Christian rap singer here. I would like you to listen to." JD listened.

The young man said to me, "If there is anything I say that displeases you, let me know." I thought that was very respectful of him. Conversation between the young man and JD started flowing. You must understand JD. She can have a conversation with anyone, no matter the age or gender.

The young man had four large metal rings on his right hand, and JD asked what they were. He said, "If anyone is considering fighting with me, they will think twice when they look at my hand. You see, years ago, I fought many fights. But I have learned that when I walk away from a fight, I am the winner. So, if someone wants to pick a fight with you or something upsets you, walk away. You are the winner when you walk away." I was wondering where this conversation was going, but in the end, it had a lesson.

This young man was dressed in black with a black hat. As I looked closer, I could see MSP (Minneapolis St. Paul) on his shirt, so I assumed he worked for the airport. He had a luggage cart next to him. JD started pushing a little on the cart, so I told her to stop

139

pushing the cart. He said the wheels are locked. Then JD pointed to his sleeve and asked, "Is your name Andrew?"

"Yes, but I go by AJ."

JD said, "I go by JD, and my sister goes by TKB."

AJ looked at TKB and said, "If you were on a sidewalk and you saw a man kick, but you didn't see what he was kicking at, and you heard a dog yelp, what would you do?"

TKB said, "I would go to protect the dog."

AJ said, "But, if you got there and the dog was biting a child, then what would you do?"

TKB said, "I would protect the child."

AJ said, "Yes, it is all in perception." From this, I learned that we sometimes find ourselves at crossroads, in a place of uncertainty, faced with perceptions borne of falsehood, misunderstanding, bias or disunity -- perceptions that do not serve us. This was another lesson AJ spoke.

AJ then said to me, "You know there is only one God, whether you are Muslim, Hindu, Christian or Jew." I agreed with him that no matter our religion, there is only one God. He then asked me what religion I was. I said I was a Lutheran, and he replied he was Catholic.

The next topic between AJ and JD was 'Minecraft,' a computer game. Since they both were familiar with this game conversation flowed between them. I certainly did not understand any of it. AJ said he knew of another Christian computer game that is like 'Minecraft' and JD you would like it too. I could tell JD was getting more comfortable with AJ because she stepped closer to him. AJ had a notebook, and JD asked what he was writing in it. AJ said he was writing a book and opened the notebook. It had colored Post-it strips in the pocket of the notebook. He gave JD several of them. She was so pleased. Then the girls saw their mother and were excited to see her. JD introduced mom to AJ and continued talking to AJ. TKB and mother went to get the baggage.

My daughter came back and said, "We better be on our way." It was obvious that JD still wanted to talk with AJ. I got up, offered my hand to AJ and said it was a pleasure to meet him and God Bless. TKB said goodbye, along with her mother. JD took the Post-it strips and asked for a pen. She wanted to write her name on it and give it to AJ. AJ gave her his pen. After writing her name she gave them to AJ. AJ looked at me, held the stickers up, and said, "Grandma, look a cross." JD had put them together in the shape of a cross. She went up to AJ and gave him a big hug. He hugged her back, and as I watched, I felt a warm, gentle feeling come over me.

As we walked toward the parking area, JD stopped and started weeping uncontrollably. Her mom asked what was wrong. JD said, "I miss AJ, and I will never see him again." She continued to cry. My daughter said, "JD, there are people we meet that we connect with and we may never see again." This is not a bad thing because we can miss them, but how wonderful to have gotten to know them, even if it was for only a short time. I embrace this moment the girls and I had. We may never know for certain what transpired, but I see no reason to dismiss the possibility that something special took place. If not an angel, then maybe God sent JD to AJ. Maybe AJ needed an unconditional warm hug from a loving little girl.

Did we entertain an angel? Perhaps. Throughout scripture, we see angels appearing to humans. I do not believe that it is different in our present day. They talk to us and can be seen. They engage in normal human activities to such a degree that we are unable to discern that they are, in fact, angels. Why would God do this? "Are not all angels ministering spirits sent to serve those who will inherit salvation?" (Hebrews 1:14)

> *We need to stop trusting only what our eyes see. If we are*
> *to see and experience everything that God wants us to see*
> *and experience, we must do so through His eyes, where*
> *our hands and feet become His hands and feet.*

TEAM JESUS

"Be alert and of sober mind. Your enemy the devil prowls around like a roaring lion looking for someone to devour." (1 Peter 5:8:)

One day I picked up my granddaughter, JD. Before going to her college cousin's home for a visit, I needed to keep my doctor's appointment. JD was always with her drawing tablet, pencils, markers, etc. While we were sitting in the waiting room, waiting for me to be called in, she started on a blank page. She drew a horizontal line to split the paper in half, upper and lower. On the top half, she wrote "Team Jesus." On the bottom half, she wrote, "Team Devil." JD began drawing objects that represented Jesus. A tree, cross, dove, bible, a church. On the bottom half, she drew objects that represented the devil. A fork, that JD has seen the devil depicted with, fire to represent hell, a broken heart.

The nurse called my name and I left my granddaughter on her own. When I returned, she showed me a new page, divided in half, left half labeled "Team Devil," right half "Team Jesus". There were eight hash marks on the side of "Team Jesus". No hash marks on the side "Team Devil." I asked her to tell me what these pages meant. She told me she went around to everyone in the waiting room and asked what team they would be on, Team Jesus or Team Devil. The result was unanimous for Jesus.

JD is not afraid to address people no matter what their age, one to a hundred. I was not shocked when she talked about what she had done, because this is her character. But I was taken by surprise about the topic of her survey. Would an adult do this? I am not a betting person, but I would bet that an adult would not.

I find that individuals shy away from conversations about Satan. She was not shy to ask whether they are for Jesus or the Devil. It is easier to keep The Enemy out of our thoughts and view. The general focus in the world is not so much on sin and judgement but on doing good and following the commandments. There seems to be less need to talk about Satan in this world. People have better things to talk about rather than which evil spirits are invading our homes, our community and our country. Families are not always Christian. It is not a general topic of conversation. It seems nobody cares.

There are times when I feel fearful, worry comes or my thoughts are not of God because of this sinful nature of mine. This is a time to speak out loud and rebuke Satan in the name of Jesus Christ. We have this power through the Holy Spirit that resides within us. You see, it must be spoken out loud because only God can hear us when we speak silently. Upon rebuking Satan, a feeling of peace will come over you.

Satan is a spiritual being. He was once holy and enjoyed heavenly honors, but because of his pride and ambition to be as God, he fell and took a host of angels with him. He is our greatest tempter and an enemy of God. Satan wants us to renounce Jesus and fall away with him. Satan is subtle and destructive, a liar and an imitator. He accuses and deceives. After you become a child of God, Satan becomes your adversary. He takes your faith in God as a personal act of opposition toward him. Therefore, he takes it upon himself to hunt you down and trap you in sin as a form of warfare. Although Satan knows that the believer's salvation cannot be lost, he finds some satisfaction in tormenting the Saints for their allegiance to the Lord. You are a child of God but that does not mean you are exempt from trials and the work of Satan.

How do we protect ourselves from Satan? "Put on the full armor of God, so that you can take your stand against the devil's schemes." (Ephesians 6:11) This armor consists of the belt, meaning truth; breastplate, meaning righteousness; shoes, meaning the readiness given by the gospel of peace; shield, meaning faith; helmet, meaning salvation; and the sword, meaning the word of God. "And pray in the Spirit on all occasions with all kinds of prayers and requests. Be alert and always keep on praying for all the Lord's people. Pray also for me, that whenever I speak, words may be given me so that I will fearlessly make known the mystery of the gospel." (Ephesians 6:18-19)

Satan not only exists but he is to be taken very seriously. Please put on the whole armor of God and stand firm in the glorious gospel of our Lord Jesus Christ. For it is He who will be victorious, and Satan who will be cast forever into the lake of fire. Praise be to God!

Be on His team today.
It is the only team that will survive.

WHAT WILL YOU TAKE TO THE CROSS?

"Then He said to them all: 'Whoever wants to be my disciple must deny themselves and take up their cross daily and follow me.'" (Luke 9:23)

n ancient times, the cross represented death. After the crucifixion of Jesus, the cross became a symbol of the risen Savior. He is no longer on the cross—He is alive! There is another reference to the cross in God's Word. "If anyone would come after me, let him deny himself and take up his cross and let him follow me." (Matthew 16:24)

During Lent, it is a good time for me to take inventory of my actions, my thoughts, my dreams and my heartaches and lay them at the foot of the cross. Oh, the list is long. There are things I once gave to my Lord, but took back, attempting to manage them on my own. If we accept that He gave His all on the cross, should we not honor Him and give Him our all?

What keeps us from giving our situation to God? "There is no fear in love. But perfect love drives out fear because fear has to do with punishment. The one who fears is not made perfect in love. We love because He first loved us." (1 John 4:18-19)

One is fear and anxiety. Do we worry what our Lord may think of us? Are we afraid of letting go of something that is a stronghold in our lives? Who wants to give up control of anything precious or even confusing, traumatic or hurtful? It is scary to let go.

We have doubts. "In spite of this, you did not trust in the Lord your God." (Deuteronomy 1:32) Do we believe that God will deliver us, heal us, guide us, protect us, take care of us and love us through the hardest parts of our lives? Do we trust that our God has that kind of power? What if His way is not our way?

There are worldly distractions. "Do not conform to the pattern of this world but be transformed by the renewing of your mind. Then you will be able to test and approve what God's will is – His good, pleasing and perfect will." (Romans 12:2) Our distractions may be our most significant barrier to the cross. Who isn't busy? We fnd ourselves overworked, overwhelmed and overscheduled. We often live chaotic lives. The reality is that we do not spend enough time in prayer or in God's word. And we do not search our souls and surrender the details of our lives to the Lord.

"Be devoted to one another in love. Honor one another above

yourselves." (Romans 12:10) We think only of ourselves. Don't we all want to do things our way? We have an inner desire to make our own choices and take care of our issues without anyone's input or help. We can handle things on our own, right? No need for allowing the Lord to take it all and carry it all. We are selfish but we can be stubborn also.

"Whoever remains stiff-necked after many rebukes will suddenly be destroyed—without remedy." (Proverbs 29:1) I think this is where the taking it back comes in. How often do we give a piece of our lives to be fixed and cleaned up? Then we decide the time is up and God did not deliver. God did not heal fast enough or resolve the conflict or crisis promptly.

Do you have pieces of your life buried behind your faith? Do you handpick what you give to God and hold the rest back? I know I have. And yet, I know that God cannot work in my life if I do not let Him. Sometimes we are so busy we forget we have an Almighty Power just waiting for our invitation. We may think we have it covered.

I am guilty as charged. I feel I am not worthy. "As a prisoner for the Lord then, I urge you to live a life worthy of the calling you have received." (Ephesians 4:1) So why do we hang on and not give everything to God?

Thanks to Jesus' resurrection, we can lay our burdens at the cross. We may do this again and again. Ask God to help you leave them at the cross. Each time you want to take them back, stop and pray.

So, I go to the cross, with it all.
And His arms are wide open.
Awaiting my offering.
He waits for yours too.
What will you lay at the foot of the cross?
He wants it all. (Author Unknown)

FINISH WELL

"For I am already being poured out like a drink offering, and the time for my departure is near. I have fought the good fight, I have finished the race, I have kept the faith. Now there is in store for me the crown of righteousness, which the Lord, the righteous Judge, will award to me on that day, and not only to me but also to all who have longed for His appearing." (2 Timothy 4:6-8)

P aul was clearly at rest, confident in the way he has spent his life. He remained calm as he faced death by decapitation. In verses 6-7 he says, "For I am already being poured out like a drink offering, and the time for my departure is near. I have fought the good fight, I have finished the race, I have kept the faith." Paul sees himself as crossing the finish line. It is easy to begin a race. It is easy to run hard for a few miles. But it is much harder to finish a long-distance race, and harder still to finish strong. Paul is telling us that the Christian life is not a sprint competition. It is a long-distance race that we need to run well, keep pace, stay focused and to finish well.

In Verse 8 Paul speaks of the future. "Now there is in store for me the crown of righteousness, which the Lord, the righteous Judge, will award to me on that day, and not only to me but also to all who have longed for his appearing." This is Paul's hope and joy as his life nears its end. He looks ahead with confidence and certainty. He shares his joy with Timothy, reminding his friend that this crown awaits not only him but also Timothy and all others who trust, serve and live for Christ.

In the last few years, I have given considerable thought about how I want to finish well. Finishing well means different things to different people. For instance, some want a cushy retirement, some want lots of toys, some wish to die painlessly. But for me finishing well means that I continue to have a relationship with God. I continue to do His work as He calls me to do. And I look forward to spending eternity with my Lord.

2 Timothy 4:7- "I have fought the good fight, I have finished the race, I have kept the faith." Paul looked back at his life in Christ and said, "I have done well." It is not that he did not make any mistakes, but he could say, "I have done what God called me to do." To do this, there are essential things we should do. Spend time with God. Be quiet and listen. Spend time reading and studying God's word. Continue to build your trust and faith in God. Stand firm in Christ.

As we run the race set before us today and tomorrow, take time to reflect on your running. Remember Paul's words to Timothy. Realize that with the Lord, you too can fight the fight, run the race and keep the faith.

It is not how you start that is important; it is how you finish.
Preparing to live and die for the glory of Christ.

FOR PERSONAL REFLECTION NOTES

_____

_____

_____

_____

_____

_____

_____

_____

_____

_____

_____

_____

_____

_____

_____

_____

FOR PERSONAL REFLECTION NOTES

FOR PERSONAL REFLECTION NOTES

Printed in the United States
by Baker & Taylor Publisher Services